CAMBRIDGE MUSIC HANDBOOKS

Chopin: The Four Ballades

CAMBRIDGE MUSIC HANDBOOKS

GENERAL EDITOR Julian Rushton

Cambridge Music Handbooks provide accessible introductions to major musical works, written by the most informed commentators in the field.

With the concert-goer, performer and student in mind, the books present essential information on the historical and musical context, the composition, and the performance and reception history of each work, or group of works, as well as critical discussion of the music.

Other published titles

Bach: Mass in B Minor JOHN BUTT

Beethoven: *Missa Solemnis* WILLIAM DRABKIN

Berg: Violin Concerto ANTHONY POPLE

Handel: *Messiah* DONALD BURROWS

Haydn: *The Creation* NICHOLAS TEMPERLEY

Haydn: String Quartets, Op. 50 W. DEAN SUTCLIFFE

Janáček: *Glagolitic Mass* PAUL WINGFIELD

Mahler: Symphony No. 3 PETER FRANKLIN

Musorgsky: *Pictures at an Exhibition* MICHAEL RUSS

Schoenberg: *Pierrot lunaire* JONATHAN DUNSBY

Schubert: *Die schöne Müllerin* SUSAN YOUENS

Schumann: Fantasie, Op. 17 NICHOLAS MARSTON

Chopin: The Four Ballades

Jim Samson
Professor of Musicology, University of Exeter

Published by the Press Syndicate of the University of Cambridge
The Pitt Building, Trumpington Street, Cambridge CB2 1RP
40 West 20th Street, New York, NY 10011–4211, USA
10 Stamford Road, Oakleigh, Melbourne 3166, Australia

© Cambridge University Press 1992

First published 1992

Printed in Great Britain at the University Press, Cambridge

A cataloguing in publication record for this book is available from the British Library

Library of Congress cataloguing in publication data
Samson, Jim.
Chopin, The Four Ballades / Jim Samson.
p. cm. – (Cambridge music handbooks)
Includes bibliographical references and index.
ISBN 0 521 38461 3 – ISBN 0 521 38615 2 (pbk)
I. Chopin, Frederick 1810–47. The Four Ballades.
II. Title.
ML410.C47P6 1992
784.2'72–dc21 91–2542 CIP

ISBN 0 521 38461 3 hardback
ISBN 0 521 38615 2 paperback

for Sue and Lois

Contents

Preface   *page* ix

Acknowledgements   x

1 *Background*   1
   Social history   1
   Stylistic history   5
   Ballade No. 1   7
   Ballades Nos. 2–4   14

2 *Genesis and reception*   20
   Sources   20
   Editions   26
   Critics   33
   Pianists   38

3 *Form and design*   45
   Ballade No. 1, Op. 23   45
   Ballade No. 2, Op. 38   51
   Ballade No. 3, Op. 47   56
   Ballade No. 4, Op. 52   62

4 *Genre*   69
   Theories   69
   Cycles   72
   Structures   76
   Narratives   81

Contents

Notes   88

Select bibliography   98

Index   101

Preface

This handbook examines the four ballades of Chopin from both historical and analytical perspectives. Chapters 1 and 2 are historical, concerned with context, origins and aftermath. Chapters 3 and 4 are analytical, concerned with formal components and functions, and with genre. There are of course meeting-points between history and analysis, even at a very basic level of investigation. Analytical tools do, after all, depend on conventional categories which emerge from history, just as historical subject-matter properly includes musical structures. But they have essentially separate areas of competence, and ask very different kinds of questions about the musical work.

As far as possible I have tried to retain some clarity about the scope and limits of these two modes of enquiry. Above all I have been anxious that the researches of the one should not be allowed to generate conclusions about the other, since such conclusions will almost certainly lack refinement. In particular analytical enquiry inclines towards a reductive view of history. It embraces contradiction in a higher synthesis, and it subordinates diversity to a quest for unity. The analytical perspective tells us above all else about today's world. Specifically it tells us what Chopin and the ballades can mean to today's world.

An historical perspective, on the other hand, will seek to explore the relationship between our world and Chopin's world, and this entails recovering something of Chopin's world, restoring to it its contemporary complexity, diversity and contradiction. It is mainly for this reason that I felt it necessary to include a substantial discussion of context in the first two parts of chapter 1. This may go some way towards countering the tendency of analytical writing first to assume that the Chopin work is a unified statement and then to gather the work, together with the rest of his output, into the fold of a notionally unified period style.

Acknowledgements

It is pleasant to record my gratitude to several people who facilitated the preparation of this book. Jeffrey Kallberg responded generously to several queries about sources; Zofia Chechlińska helped me find my way through nineteenth-century editions; Katharine Ellis shared her expertise on nineteenth-century French criticism; James Methuen-Campbell and Tim Mobbe helped with early recordings, and Rosemary Meikle with bibliographical materials. I am grateful to my colleague Nicholas Marston, who offered valuable advice and encouragement, and to the Chopin authority John Rink, who read the manuscript and commented helpfully on the general structure of the book and on numerous points of detail.

1

Background

Social history

The First Scherzo and First Ballade were composed during Chopin's early years in Paris. The exact dates of their composition have not been determined reliably, but it is probable that neither work was begun before 1833. Indeed on stylistic and other evidence it seems likely that they were drafted not long before their publication in 1835 and 1836 respectively.[1] Whatever their precise dates of composition, the Scherzo and Ballade have special significance within Chopin's output. They were the first of his extended compositions to turn aside from the genres of post-classical popular concert music (variation sets, rondos and 'brilliant' concertos) as well as those of so-called 'Viennese' Classicism (multi-movement sonatas and chamber works).[2] In the Scherzo and Ballade Chopin followed a special path. He drew sustenance from classical and post-classical traditions, but remained essentially independent of both – to the point of establishing new genres. There is of course a stylistic background to Chopin's achievement in these two works, a range of early influences that left their trace even as they were transcended. But there is also a wider social background. Some of the enabling factors were products of Chopin's unique position within the social world of early nineteenth-century pianism. Here too he followed a special path.

Born in 1810, his early development as a composer took place in Warsaw during the 1820s. Warsaw was by no means a leading cultural centre in the early nineteenth century, but – at least until the 1830 insurrection – it registered something of the major change then taking place more widely in music and music-making. That change, reflecting a fundamental reshaping of European society, penetrated into many aspects of the infrastructure of musical life, and only some of its manifestations may be outlined here. In essence the musical centre of gravity shifted from court to city, as a politically emergent middle class increasingly shaped and directed formal culture. This central transformation carried with it many ancillary transformations – in the professional status of composers and performers, in the social make-up of audiences, in tastes and in repertories. The change was associated in particular with the institution of the public concert and with its corollary, the rise of the piano.

Already by the 1820s – Chopin's formative years – classical keyboard traditions were overshadowed by a repertory of post-classical piano music associated with the flamboyant, cosmopolitan and above all commercial concert life of a newly influential middle class. This repertory, clearly focused on the virtuoso pianist-composer, exulted almost fetishistically in the powers of an instrument now firmly established. The virtuoso played mainly his own works, performing them at benefit concerts (his own and those of other artists), *matinées* and *soirées*, and tailoring his programmes and his compositional style to the needs of an audience seeking above all novelty and display. The pianist-composer was inevitably an entrepreneur, closely meshed into a promotional network which included publishers, critics and piano manufacturers. The piano became a powerful symbol of the commodity character increasingly attached to music in a post-patronal age. And this was reinforced by its growing domestic role within bourgeois society, eliciting a repertory of *Trivialmusik* which formed the mainstay of the publisher's income.

Chopin's early years in Warsaw were geared towards a career as pianist-composer within this milieu. His major compositions adopted the genres favoured by other virtuoso-composers, notably in the three early works for piano and orchestra – a variation set, potpourri and rondo, characteristically based (respectively) on a well-known operatic aria (Variations on *Là ci darem la mano*), a string of folk melodies (*Fantasy on Polish Airs*) and a so-called 'national' dance (*Rondo à la Krakoviak*). Together with the two piano concertos, these were well suited to the public concert of the day, just as the solo piano works, mainly rondos and dance pieces, were appropriate to the *soirée* and *matinée*. There were also 'private' works such as the Sonata Op. 4 and the Piano Trio Op. 8, markedly different in idiom from the concert pieces. And this very distinction between public and private styles was itself entirely in keeping with the normal practice of the virtuoso composer.

When Chopin arrived in Paris in September 1831, following an unproductive nine-month stay in Vienna, this orientation towards conventional public pianism had already been rejected. He did not abandon the concert platform, but he remained aloof from the commercial concert world of the pianist-composer and his public appearances were few and far between.[3] At the same time he did not seek to establish himself as a composer of major ambition by turning to the prestigious genres of opera, symphony or chamber music. Despite his avoidance of the concert platform, he remained committed to 'pianists' music'[4] and was invariably judged as a pianist-composer, playing almost exclusively his own music when he graced the salons.[5] That it was a special path was well recognised at the time. A reviewer of the newly published Waltzes Op. 64 remarked that where other pianists would promote their music by 'announc[ing] a concert or see[ing] company at Erard's or Broadwood's ... M. Chopin ... quietly publishes *2* [*sic*] *Waltzes*'.[6]

It is worth expanding a little on this special path, since it had major implications for musical style in the mature works, including the ballades. Chopin did not, like Hummel, divide his creative activities cleanly between public display works for the piano and more serious private compositions in classical genres. Nor did he, like Liszt, 'progress' from the career of virtuoso-composer to the dual career of modernist composer and classical recitalist. Rather he accepted the stylistic framework of public virtuosity and salon music but went on to elevate their traditions to unprecedented levels of artistic excellence. His achievement was to refine and give new substance to the conventions of popular pianism, enriching those conventions by drawing upon elements from other – and weightier – musical worlds. In this way he achieved a unique synthesis of the public and private, the popular and the significant. When it came to extended forms, that meant a synthesis of the formal methods of popular concert music – above all the alternation of bravura figuration and melodic paragraphs based on popular genres – and the sonata-based designs and organic tonal structures of the Austro-German tradition. The First Scherzo and First Ballade were the earliest fruits of that synthesis.

When Chopin wrote these works in the mid-1830s, further changes were taking place in piano music and in public concerts. The world of popular pianism, centred on the benefit concert and salon, was already fading around this time. And as it did so two different, polemically related, strands of music-making emerged, their profiles well defined against the background of a commercial concert life. Together they represented a further stage in the consolidation of a middle-class culture. On the one hand there were 'modern' works flamed by the spirit of Romanticism – by an expressive aesthetic of which the piano proved an ideal advocate, in both heroic and intimate modes. At its most ambitious this repertory amounted to an incipient avant-garde. On the other hand there were prestigious classical concerts centred on what was gradually becoming a standard repertory, a constructed tradition which served to validate a newly emerging middle-class establishment. Underlying this contrast between an emerging modernism and a strengthening classicism was a shared sense of the dignity of the musical work in marked contrast to the ephemeral status assigned to music within a commercial concert life.

Chopin's mature music, firmly grounded in the post-classical concert music of the 1820s, was influenced by both these developments in the 1830s and 1840s. His response to a romantic aesthetic undoubtedly contributed to the qualitative change in his musical style in the early Paris years, to the new 'tone' of works like the First Scherzo and First Ballade. Admittedly Chopin had little interest in the surface manifestations of Romanticism in music. He shared none of the contemporary enthusiasm for the descriptive, denotative powers of music, remaining committed to so-called absolute music in an age dominated by programmes and descriptive titles. Yet he did register the romantic climate at the deeper level of an expressive aesthetic, where the musical work might become a 'fragment of autobiography'.[7] In the early 1830s Chopin's music acquired an intensity, a passion, at times a terrifying power, which can rather easily suggest an inner life whose turmoils were lived out in music. It was in part this expressive imperative, allied to a sense of the pretension and ambition of the musical work, which transformed a post-classical into a romantic idiom.

Chopin was widely counted among the progressives of early nineteenth-century music. At the same time, like many other progressives in an age of growing historical awareness, he took much of his creative inspiration from an earlier age, specifically from Bach and Mozart. The transformation of their inheritance was a further important catalyst of his stylistic maturity in the early 1830s. Yet for all his classical sympathies Chopin played little part in the establishment of those 'historical concerts' and recitals which promoted a classical repertory in the 1830s and 1840s, gradually transforming concert life into a structure recognisably similar to our own. While he continued to play his own music, pianist-composers such as Liszt and Moscheles increasingly programmed 'standard' works by other composers.[8] Bach and Beethoven were especially favoured.

In due course Chopin's music itself permeated this steadily expanding standard repertory. Indeed it was already beginning to do so during his lifetime, partly through the persuasive advocacy of Liszt, who regularly programmed the études and mazurkas. The major extended works took longer to establish themselves as seminal items in the classical canon. But already by the early 1840s they were beginning to take their place in the programmes of benefits by other pianists, notably pupils and associates such as Charles Hallé and the young Carl Filtsch. Both gave concerts in London in the summer of 1843 and their Chopin playing was highly praised. Of Filtsch, who included the First Ballade in at least one of his programmes, *The Athenaeum* remarked 'we have had no pleasure greater than hearing him in Chopin's music ... [which] is fast advancing in popularity in London'. Hallé played the First Scherzo, and his reading of it was described as 'fanciful, elegant, capricious, sentimental, without a trace of that sickliness to which the music would invite the half cultivated'.[9] It is to such concerts and such reviews that we can trace the beginning of a long tradition of Chopin interpretation and criticism which has continued until our own time.

Stylistic history

The music of Chopin's Warsaw years, composed between 1817 and 1830, may be related rather closely to the popular 'pianists' music' of the early nineteenth century. This repertory was the foundation upon which his mature music was built, and its conventions were never entirely rejected, even in the most ambitious works. The early polonaises, variations and rondos are in the brilliant manner,[10] with specific debts to Hummel and Weber in the exuberant ornamentation of the polonaises and the bravura figuration of the rondos. The practices of contemporary improvisation, an essential part of the pianist-composer's armoury, left a clear mark on much of this music. The Sonata Op. 4 and Piano Trio Op. 8, on the other hand, employ the classical idiom commonly associated with the 'private' works of pianist-composers, and it is worth noting that the Trio was composed for private aristocratic performance at Antonin.[11] The simpler dance pieces – mazurkas and waltzes – form another group, avoiding virtuosic embellishment and bravura figuration, and lending themselves well to domestic music-making. Finally there is the E minor Nocturne, which registers clearly the lyrical pianism of John Field and already hints at ways of developing beyond it.

The Vienna and early Paris years (1830–32) witnessed a gradual but unmistakable transformation of Chopin's musical style. No doubt this was closely allied to changes in his personal attitudes and circumstances, as he faced up to Vienna's indifference, to Poland's developing tragedy – culminating in the suppression of the 1830 insurrection – and to his own increasing disenchantment with the proposed career of a composer-pianist. Whatever the cause, the change of tone is apparent in different ways in the Op. 6 and Op. 7 Mazurkas, the Op. 9 Nocturnes and the Op. 10 Etudes.

The nocturnes and études in particular marked an important advance in technique and expression. It was above all in these pieces that the conventions and materials of post-classical concert music were refashioned and transcended. In the second of the Op. 9 Nocturnes the vocally inspired ornamental devices employed by Field and others were refined and ultimately absorbed into melodic substance. Far from a virtuosic embellishment of melody, as in the brilliant style, ornamentation here plays an evolutionary, even developmental, role. It is at once an expressive enhancement of the original, a tension-building strategy and a means of highlighting the main structural elements of the music. The resulting fusion of ornament and melody into a single continuously unfolding, chromatically curving line easily transcended the conventional practice of early nineteenth-century pianism, while at the same time *recovering* something of the characteristic melodic style of a Mozart slow movement. Forged here in the early nocturnes, Chopin's ornamental melody would come to full fruition in the major works of his later years, not least in the reprise of the Fourth Ballade.

In the Op. 10 Etudes Chopin looked again at the conventional figuration of early nineteenth-century pianism, allowing well-established patterns to take on fresh meaning. And if there was a single factor which helped it to do so it was the influence of Bach. In conversation with Eugène Delacroix, Chopin maintained that counterpoint should lie right at the heart of stable musical structures.[12] In some ways his own contrapuntal style achieved for the piano what Bach had achieved for earlier keyboard instruments, reinterpreting traditional techniques in terms of the unique qualities of the instrument. Chopin's counterpoint takes its starting-point from the capacity of the piano to layer voices through shaded dynamics, allowing lines to emerge and recede imperceptibly from the texture. Characteristically a figuration will embrace tiny linear motives on a foreground level while outlining larger linear progressions (usually by means of an organic chromaticism) on a middle-ground level. In both respects there is a contrapuntal enrichment of conventional patterns which is very much in the spirit, and often in the manner, of Bach. Here, in the Op. 10 Etudes, Chopin's characteristic figuration reached maturity. It would become an important component of all four ballades, and it achieved thematic status in No. 2.

There was a further, and perhaps more fundamental, development of style in Chopin's music of the Vienna and early Paris years. Already during his Warsaw period he began to acquire a long-range harmonic vision which enabled him to gain structural control over the materials of the brilliant style, habitually presented in highly sectionalised formal designs which alternate lyrical and figurative paragraphs. Characteristically such alternating paragraphs would be relatively self-contained, with clearly-defined harmonic divisions. Chopin's achievement was to subordinate them to more extended over-arching tonal spans, embracing formal contrast within a higher tonal synthesis and ensuring a priority of tonal structure over sectionalised formal design.[13] At the same time he did not entirely lose sight of the formal methods of the brilliant style. The starting-point for even his most sophisticated later works often remained an alternation of melody and figuration, as both style-critical and genetic analysis indicates.[14] The formal process of post-classical concert music may indeed have been transcended, but it was also remembered.

These stylistic transformations registered a fundamental change in Chopin's whole approach to composition, a change which might be summarised crudely as an investment in the musical work rather than the musical performance. As we have noted, it was a change for which there was a wider context in the musical climate of the 1830s, yet its realisation in Chopin's music remained in the end triumphantly specific. Other composers, notably Liszt in some works, attempted to turn the forms and conventions of the popular repertory to ambitious account,[15] but it is difficult to find any real parallel to the project of renovation upon which Chopin embarked in his early Paris years. It amounted to nothing less than a thorough-going reworking of the popular repertory – its materials, its forms and ultimately its genres.

It is conspicuous that after 1832 Chopin largely abandoned the genres most favoured within post-classical concert music. Following the Rondo Op. 16 and the *Variations brillantes* Op. 12 his inclination was to employ genre titles that had clear associations within popular pianism, but whose conventional meanings were either narrowly circumscribed or loosely defined. His own music then invested weight and significance to these genre titles, even to the point of establishing new genres. In this respect the music of the early Paris years gave substance to the dance piece of functional entertainment (the waltz as much as the Polish dances) as well as to the étude, the chief vehicle for didactic music. At the same time it gave sharper definition to genre titles such as 'nocturne' and 'impromptu', retaining conventional associations with vocal transcription and imitation (the nocturne) and with improvisation (the impromptu), but subordinating these associations to the establishment and consolidation of clearly-defined genres.[16] And it is against this background of generic renovation that Chopin's approach to single-movement extended structures in the First Scherzo and First Ballade needs to be considered.

Ballade No. 1

The achievements of the early Paris years – in melody, figuration and harmony – informed and enabled the Scherzo and Ballade. Yet the two works established very different ways of building upon those achievements. Of the two, the Scherzo is the closer to the formal methods of the brilliant style, characteristically enclosing a popular melody (possibly based on a Polish carol) within a figuration, and aligning this basic contrast to a conventional formal pattern (schema). At the same time the dynamic energy and sheer power of the figuration (qualitatively different from anything Chopin composed during his Warsaw years) and the subtlety with which it yields first to motive and then to harmony leave us in no doubt that the brilliant style has been transcended, and that the genre title 'scherzo' has been entirely rethought.[17]

The Ballade followed a different course, albeit proceeding from a similar stylistic base. Unlike the Scherzo, it rests solidly on the foundations of a sonata-form design, couching its materials in a through-composed, harmonically directional structure where variation and transformation are seminal functions, integration and synthesis essential goals. It may be helpful to present the position baldly, if a little over-simply. Viewed as a whole the scherzos and ballades embody a synthesis of the post-classical brilliant style and the classical sonata-form archetype. In relation to this the First Scherzo leans towards the brilliant style and the First Ballade towards the sonata principle. Later pieces in both genres allow for some interpenetration of schemata, but they preserve the basic difference in orientation established in the two pioneering works.

There was of course a major shift in style between the sonata-form elements of Chopin's Warsaw-period works (especially the Op. 4 Sonata and the Piano Trio) and those of the First Ballade. In the Ballade, sonata-based formal functions have clearly been reinterpreted in the light of a particular dramatic and expressive aim, a 'plot archetype' shared by other early nineteenth-century works.[18] Above all the structure is end-weighted, with a rising intensity curve culminating in a reprise which is more apotheosis than synthesis. In this context the bravura closing section, marked off from the work by a change of metre as well as by its non-thematic character, has an essential and highly specific formal function. Yet even this gesture (including the change of metre) has origins in the brilliant style, notably in the applause-seeking finales so characteristic of fantasies and variation sets by pianist-composers. And this is only one of several ways in which elements of post-classical concert music transformed the normative practice of classical sonata form in this work.

Another instance of transformation concerns thematic characterisation. The genre of the classical sonata is defined by thematic character as well as by formal function, and in this respect Chopin's early piano sonata is conformant.

Example 1

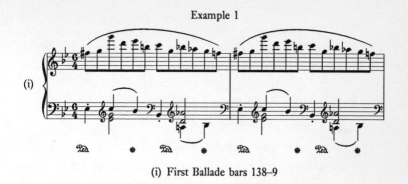

(i)

(i) First Ballade bars 138–9

(ii)

(ii) Three Waltzes Op. 34: No. 1 bars 33–6

So, in less obvious ways, are his three mature sonatas. In contrast, the themes in the Ballade spell out the work's continuing links with the world of popular pianism, where thematic material was commonly grounded in popular genres. The pivotal episode in E♭ major at bar 138 is the most obvious point at which a popular genre emerges into the foreground of the Ballade. With its arc-shaped moto perpetuo arabesques this episode immediately invokes the characteristic phraseology of the Chopin waltz, a phraseology which had been defined in Op. 18, the first of the 'Paris' waltzes (also in E♭ major), and would later be confirmed in the Three Waltzes Op. 34. The affinity is obvious even in an informal inspection (Ex. 1). And this explicit association sheds light in turn on the two main themes of the Ballade. Subsumed by the compound duple metre of its first theme are the basic features of a slow waltz (the two-bar groupings of several of Chopin's waltzes often suggest compound duple), while underlying the second theme we may already detect the hazy outlines of a barcarolle, clearer still in the reprise of the theme. The contrasted rhythmic profile of the two main themes (Ex. 2) is an important dimension of the Ballade.

The presentation of themes related to popular genres within a sonata-form

Example 2

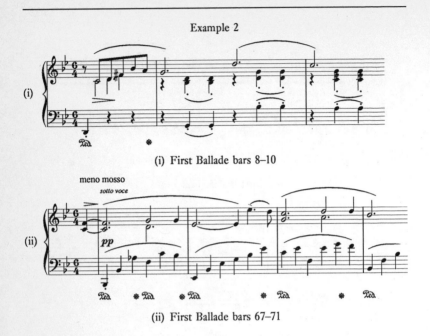

(i) First Ballade bars 8–10

(ii) First Ballade bars 67–71

framework is perfectly symptomatic of Chopin's larger achievement as a composer. By elevating popular traditions to a higher level of creativity he demonstrated that even in an age intent on prising apart the accessible and the sophisticated there need be no contradiction between them. And precisely because of its more ambitious context the popular genre took on an additional layer of meaning in Chopin, quite unlike anything in the brilliant style. In the widest sense of the term an ironic mode was introduced.[19]

The First Ballade was of course much more than an outcome of Chopin's refinement and enrichment of the traditions of popular pianism. Simply by using the title 'ballade' for a piano piece he invoked a very much wider range of reference in both musical and literary contexts. Contemporary dictionaries and music lexicons establish clearly that the connotations of the title 'ballade' were exclusively vocal until the 1840s.[20] And in this connection it is significant that early advertisements for Op. 23 included the description *ohne Worte* (without words),[21] establishing immediately a connection with vocal music. The opening of the work makes this connection explicit through the tonally inductive 'recitative' which precedes the G minor 'aria'. And there are telling associations to be made more generally with the repertory of early nineteenth-century opera.[22] French operas in particular used the term 'ballade' to describe

10

a simple narrative song (usually strophic), and very often this was couched in the same compound duple metre employed by Chopin in Op. 23 and in the later ballades.

The title 'ballade' also invites comparison with early nineteenth-century song. Here the instrumental ballade might be presumed to stand in the same relation to a ballad setting as the song without words to a vocal romance. And again it is notable that ballad settings by Schubert, Loewe and others were frequently presented in a 'narrative' 6/8 or 6/4 metre, borrowing freely from a convention commonly associated with pastoral music of the eighteenth and early nineteenth centuries. The connotations are explicit. Put simply, the lyric poem and its musical setting expressed an emotion, while the ballad and its musical setting told a story. For contemporary audiences this was an inescapable resonance of Chopin's title 'ballade'. Indeed such associations were increasingly part of the critical discourse about instrumental music in general in the 1830s. 'We have always valued instrumental music as it has *spoken to us*', wrote Chorley in 1834, 'and can never listen to the delightful works of Beethoven, Mozart, Haydn, Ries, Onslow, and some others, without having their sentiment – nay, when we are in a fanciful humour – their *story*, as clearly impressed upon our minds as if it had been told in words.'[23]

Chorley's reference to 'sentiment' and 'story' highlights a central preoccupation of an emerging romantic aesthetic in music, a preoccupation with the expressive and denotative powers of musical discourse. Within the popular repertory this took the form of a revival of baroque pictorialism. There was a plethora of descriptive pieces, especially battle pieces, in the early nineteenth century, their formal and expressive events dictated in entirely specific ways by an unfolding narrative.[24] Some of these were even published as musical 'serials', so that their narrative unfolded over a period of several weeks or months.[25] Naturally among progressive composers programmatic interests were cultivated with much greater pretension. For Berlioz, Liszt and Schumann the world of literature was anything but a dilettante's playground. It was an all-important store of potential 'subjects', which might generate directly, and often at deep levels of structure, the essential shape of a musical work. There was also a sense, validated in Hegel's influential aesthetics, that music might be dignified and elevated through its contacts with poetry.

Again it was in the 1830s that such interests surfaced. There can be little doubt that the earlier explosion of romantic literature played a catalytic role, stimulating composers directly, and playing some part in promoting (or insinuating) the idea that they should be so stimulated by literature in the first place. Unlike most of their predecessors, the early romantic composers were

11

men of a wide general culture, as the titles and programmes of their music indicate. Already by 1835, when Chopin almost certainly composed the First Ballade, Berlioz had written instrumental works inspired by Shakespeare, Schumann had established a lifelong creative relationship (some of it concealed from the public) with the prose of Jean Paul and Hoffmann, and Liszt had composed a major piano work inspired by the poetry of Lamartine. In all there was an attempt to weave literary ideas into the substance of a musical work, establishing a dialogue between dramatic or poetic themes and the inherited forms and genres of instrumental music.

Chopin, on the other hand, avoided such programmatic associations, shunning any attempt to express the world of external reality (as opposed to an inner emotional reality) through his music. By temperament he was anything but the 'romantic composer' of popular imagination, and he shared little of his fellow composers' knowledge of, and enthusiasm for, the other arts. There were, it is true, contacts with the Polish poets Cyprian Norwid and Adam Mickiewicz and with the great French painter Eugène Delacroix, but it is difficult to see how these could have shaped or directed in any significant way the course of his musical development. He avoided opera and programme music and his few contributions to the art song, that quintessential romantic genre, only served to emphasise that he was at least as close to an earlier classical aesthetic as to the spirit of Romanticism.

At the same time it would be misleading to suggest that Chopin's use of the title 'ballade' excluded its obvious literary associations. In the early nineteenth century the medieval and, more particularly, folk genre had been effectively reinvented for romantic literature and its connotative values were specific and widely recognised. By describing Op. 23 as a 'ballade' Chopin inevitably made a gesture in this direction, and in doing so he established some point of contact with the literary preoccupations of his contemporaries. But it is entirely characteristic that literary inspiration should have been channelled into a piano piece with a deliberately generalised rather than an explicitly programmatic title. In very much the same way Chopin's commitment to an expressive aesthetic was filtered into the piano nocturne rather than rendered specific in the art song. And even his nationalism was expressed through a renovation of the 'salon' dance piece rather than through opera or programmatic reference. In all three cases he drew upon prevailing ideas from the non-musical world without allowing those ideas to challenge the essential condition of absolute music.

This has a bearing on the endless speculation about the influence of Mickiewicz's ballads on the Chopin ballades. It is indeed distinctly possible

Example 3

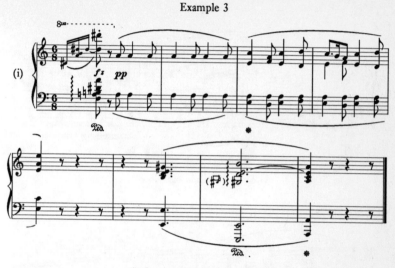

(i) Second Ballade bars 197–204

(ii) Nocturne Op. 37 No. 2 bars 132–9

that these poems may have played some part in Chopin's creative process, as Schumann reported.[26] But they cannot be part of the aesthetic property of the music itself, since no specific designate is part of its subject or content, in the way that Lamartine's poetry is part of the subject (because it is part of the

Example 4

(i) Second Ballade bars 46–8

(ii) Etudes Op. 25: No. 11 bars 3–5

title) of Liszt's *Harmonies poétiques et religieuses*. The title 'ballade' signifies no particular programme, then, but it does invite the listener to interpret musical relationships at least partly in the terms of a literary narrative, even if this can only be at the level of metaphor. It is not so much the intrinsic qualities of the musical work which may suggest a narrative, but our predisposition – given the genre title – to construct a narrative from the various ways in which purely musical events are transformed through time. Such a musical narrative would be based on the generic character and interplay of themes, on the transformation of conventional formal successions and on the organisation of large-scale tonal relationships.

Ballades Nos 2–4

The period between the publication of the First Ballade in 1836 and the composition of the Fourth Ballade in 1842 was one of relative stability in

Example 5. Meyerbeer *Robert le diable* Act I Ballade

Chopin's life. These were his most productive years as a composer, and they witnessed some of his finest music, including of course the three later ballades. There are generic invariants which relate these works to the First Ballade. But there are also stylistic invariants which relate them to their more immediate period setting. Inevitably they have much in common with the other single-movement extended works composed during these years, since all were concerned to find new contexts for the sonata-form archetype. But parallels extend beyond generalised formal and tonal procedures into more detailed fingerprints of style. The main theme of the Second Ballade, for instance, is closely related to part of the G major Nocturne Op. 37 No. 2, composed at more or less the same time in 1838–9, and the affinity is strengthened by very similar thematic treatments in the final bars of the two pieces (Ex. 3). The second 'theme' of the Ballade – in effect a figuration – might equally be compared to the eleventh of the Op. 25 Etudes, the so-called 'Winter Wind', in the same key of A minor, notable for what Camille Bourniquel described as its 'irresistible unleashing of power';[27] and the two figurations are approached in a very similar way, as Ex. 4 indicates.

It is worth focusing a little more on the basic character of this material. As in the First Ballade there are rather specific links with a popular repertory. The opening theme is unmistakably a siciliano, carrying with it a wealth of pastoral associations which are strengthened by its F major tonality. Niecks referred to its links with 'the people's storehouse of song'.[28] There are obvious affinities with some of the 'pastoral rondos' which were so popular in early nineteenth-century piano music, as well as with a repertory of contemporary French opera which was well known to Chopin. In particular Raimbaud's Ballade from Act I of Meyerbeer's immensely popular opera *Robert le diable* is a tempting point of comparison (Ex. 5).[29] Chopin admired the work and in 1832–3 he collaborated with Auguste Franchomme in setting a medley of its themes for cello and piano.[30] The Meyerbeer Ballade has a double stanzaic structure not unlike that of the Chopin, and it is worth noting that its description of an innocent Norman princess threatened by the warrior Robert, 'le favori fidèle de Satan', is strikingly similar to the theme of Mickiewicz's poem *Switeź*, a putative inspiration for Chopin's Second Ballade.

Equally the sharply contrasted figuration reaches beyond the parallel with Op. 25 No. 11 to suggest a more generalised background in the figuration of the brilliant style. And however transcendent the musical quality, this generic contrast of a siciliano tune and a bravura figuration is entirely in the manner of the popular repertory. Even the much-discussed two-key scheme of the Ballade finds a context in this repertory, notably in works such as Kalkbrenner's Grand Fantasy Op. 68 or Hummel's Fantasy Op. 18, the latter following exactly the same tonal plan as the Chopin, a double sequence of E♭ major and G minor, until its final extended tierce de picardie. The two-key scheme is in short as much a residue of the past as a premonition of the future.[31]

Such generic allusions and intertextual associations, stronger here than in the other three ballades, encourage us to locate within the Second Ballade a rather specific dramaturgy, if not a 'narrative'. The work retains from the sonata-form archetype a basic thematic and tonal dualism, but sharpens that dualism into something approaching a dramatic conflict of genres, as the 'siciliano' and 'étude' collide forcefully, interact dramatically and ultimately force a dénouement. It is no coincidence that this Ballade should be the one most often cited in connection with a programmatic inspiration, and there is evidence (albeit inconclusive) that such an inspiration did indeed exist. Aside from Schumann's reporting, there is a reference in the correspondence of Henryk Probst to the 'pilgrim's ballade', a possible link with Mickiewicz.[32] More precise documentation has proved elusive, but tradition has it that the Second Ballade was inspired by Mickiewicz's ballad *Switeź*, which recounts how the maidens of a Polish village were besieged by Russian soldiers. They pray that they might be swallowed by the earth, and when their wish is granted they are transformed into beautiful flowers which adorn the site of the village.

It would be rather easy to map this plot on to the musical processes of the Ballade, if Chopin had legitimised such an exercise through a title or programme. Several levels of parallelism suggest themselves for the basic contrast between melody and figuration. Mickiewicz's opening five stanzas depict the beauty of the pastoral setting by the lake before contrasting that with the terrible things which reportedly take place in the lake at night. Alternatively the innocence of the Polish maidens may be contrasted with the advent of the Russian soldiers. Yet it is scarcely necessary to engage in these exercises. Given the music's range of musical associations, we do not need a Mickiewicz poem to 'read' the Second Ballade's narrative of innocence under threat, a narrative which presents in turn confrontation, mediation and transformation. The generic contrast (siciliano–étude) and the two-key scheme are integral components of that narrative.

The Third Ballade was composed two years after the second in 1841, one of Chopin's most prolific years. It owes something to the First Ballade (its formal process, even down to the pivotal waltz theme) and something to the second (the generic character of its themes), but in the end it establishes its own rather specific character, akin to Schubert in the song-like (as opposed to aria-like) lyricism of its opening theme and in the careful symmetries of its periodic phrasing.[33] On closer examination, however, the Ballade's opening theme reveals a complexity and density of thought which prefigures the formal ambiguities and powerfully innovatory thematic treatments of the later stages of the work, for which there are few precedents in Chopin's earlier music. Already in these later stages of the Ballade there are hints of the remarkable achievements of his final years.

There is a consensus among commentators that a third period in Chopin's creative life began around 1842, though it was less an abrupt change of direction than an extension of practices already present in his music to the point at which changes became qualitative. One notable indicator of change was a dramatic decline in his rate of production.[34] It seems that composition became more difficult for Chopin in the 1840s. His flow of ideas was undiminished but he became more and more self-critical about committing himself to a final version of a piece and entrusting it to paper, as the manuscript sources of his later music reveal clearly. 'He spends days of nervous tension and almost terrifying desperation', wrote the novelist George Sand, Chopin's partner for some ten years. 'He alters and retouches the same passages endlessly and paces up and down like a madman.' Undoubtedly Chopin engaged in a fundamental rethinking of his craft at this time, among other things examining counterpoint treatises by Cherubini and Kastner.[35] Evidence of this rethinking is easily found in the music of 1842, including the Fourth Ballade.

For one thing there is a new fluidity and unpredictability in the formal

Example 6

(i) Hummel Fantasy Op. 18 bars 613–22

(ii) Chopin Fourth Ballade bars 198–211

organisation of the later works, a tendency for the music to open unexpectedly into new developmental areas and to blend elements of different formal archetypes in a purposefully ambiguous way. The extraordinary formal richness and powerful goal-directed momentum of the Fourth Ballade are characteristic, in particular the subtle, almost imperceptible, return of the introductory material and the blend of sonata elements and variations. Another striking aspect of the later music is the restraint with which Chopin ornaments his melodic substance – a far cry indeed from the exuberant, permissive ornamentation of the early Warsaw music. The decorative flowering of the first theme in the reprise of the Fourth Ballade makes its expressive and structural point precisely because of a calculated restraint in the earlier stages of the work. In the later music there is also a more adventurous approach to counterpoint, expressed partly through greater independence of part-movement (often involving unorthodox dissonance in the interest of linear values) and partly through the seamless absorption of canonic elements into the musical flow. Here too the Fourth Ballade affords us examples in the polyphonic treatments of its main themes, culminating in the canonic writing which introduces the reprise at bar 135.

In some ways the sequence of events in this reprise – a canonic working of the theme followed by a fioritura variation – is neatly symptomatic of Chopin's relation to popular pianism. On one level it represents a triumphant synthesis of the very different worlds of strict counterpoint (Bach) and ornamental bel canto (Italian opera). On another it is a characteristic succession of contemporary improvisation, where the theme (on occasion supplied by an audience) would be played 'straight', then processed in various ways, including canonic-fugal and cantabile-decorative styles. Cortot goes so far as to describe the work as a kind of 'stylised improvisation'. For all its transcendent quality, then, the Fourth Ballade retains its links with popular pianism, not least in its final stages. The passage which precedes the bravura closing section (bars 198–210) has extraordinary dramatic power, arguably unprecedented in Chopin's music. At the same time it is an unmistakable echo of Hummel's practice in the closing pages of his Op. 18 Fantasy (Ex. 6).

1842 was a year for culminating statements. The last of the scherzos also dated from that year, as did the last and greatest of the polonaises – the A♭ major, Op. 53 – and, more trivially, the last of the impromptus. Like the Scherzo and the Polonaise, the Fourth Ballade both confirmed its genre and inaugurated a new period in Chopin's creative life, paving the way for a yet more exploratory, even at times an experimental, approach to musical materials and their organisation. In works such as the Berceuse, the Barcarolle and the Polonaise-fantaisie Chopin seemed to reach a new plateau of transcendent creative achievement, truly a 'last style'.[36]

2

Genesis and reception

Sources

Like many pianist-composers, Chopin allowed his first thoughts about a work to take shape at the piano. George Sand described the process vividly – and in a manner which emphasises its links with improvisation – when she remarked that 'invention came to his piano, sudden, complete, sublime'.[1] As a result the larger structure and much of the detailed working of a piece would usually be in place and held *in intellectu* before he ever put pen to paper. When he finally did so, it might be to sketch some of the basic ideas as a preliminary to making a fair copy. This represents *Stage I* of a source-chain for several Chopin works. It was often by-passed, however, and it should be noted that there are no extant sketches for any of the ballades. Manuscript sources so described in the literature have been incorrectly classified.[2]

Next Chopin would prepare a fair copy, which usually functioned as a *Stichvorlage* or engraver's manuscript. These are often 'dirty', with changes made either at the time of writing or later (sometimes in a different pen), involving heavy tessellations and revisions on the third staff above or below the main text. In some instances Chopin abandoned the manuscript to begin again, and such 'rejected public manuscripts',[3] strictly speaking *Stage II* of a source-chain, are often valuable documents. There is one such abandoned manuscript for the Fourth Ballade. The other main autograph sources for the ballades served as the *Stichvorlagen* (*Stage III*) for at least one of the original editions. Due mainly to the length of the works, there are no presentation manuscripts, *Stage IV* for some shorter pieces.

Chopin's music – from 1834 onwards – was published 'simultaneously' (or nearly so) in France, Germany and England, a practice (common enough at the time) designed to avoid piracy due to the variation in copyright laws in different countries. In most cases the French publisher was Maurice Schlesinger, the German Breitkopf & Härtel and the English Wessel. Chopin usually gave his fair copy directly to Schlesinger, proof-reading himself in early and late periods and often (but not always) relying on others to do so in the intervening period 1835–41. Occasionally a copy, notably by his childhood friend Julian Fontana, would be sent instead. With Breitkopf & Härtel he sent proof-sheets from the French edition until late 1835, after which he sent manuscripts, though until 1842 (when Fontana left for America) these were often copies (*Stage V*).[4] Although Chopin took great care to ensure that a correct text was sent to Leipzig, he had no further control over the German edition once it had left his hands. This was also true of the English editions. His dealings with Wessel were in any case rather complicated.[5] Until 1843 proofs, copies and autographs were variously sent, after which autograph manuscripts seem to have been the norm.

Due to these various publishing options there are numerous textual differences between the three first editions, which collectively represent *Stage VI*. Moreover Chopin annotated certain of the (mainly French) first editions belonging to pupils. There are several collections containing such glosses, including Ludwika Jędrzejewicz's three-volume collection, Camilla O'Meara Dubois's three-volume collection and – most importantly – Jane Stirling's seven-volume collection.[6] The status of these glosses – a stage in the source-chain which post-dates the first editions (*Stage VII*) – is deeply problematical,[7] though there are relatively few such annotations on the ballades.

The genesis of the G minor Ballade (No. 1) has traditionally been given as 1830–1,[8] probably the result of unreliable evidence from Schlesinger in a newspaper interview of *ca* 1860.[9] A much later date is indicated on stylistic grounds and also – at least for the surviving autograph – on paper evidence. The autograph is the *Stichvorlage* prepared for Schlesinger and its paper type is identical to that of other manuscripts certainly prepared in 1835–6, including the autograph of Op. 26. Lengthy gestation periods were not in any case characteristic of Chopin and we can assume that he followed his normal practice of beginning a work a year or at most two years before its publication.

The autograph[10] has a title page with the title and dedication (à M. le baron Stockhausen) in Chopin's hand.[11] The opus number, the names of the three publishers and the plate number of the French edition (MS 1928) are also on the title page, but in another hand.[12] As usual with Chopin's *Stichvorlagen* there are numerous corrections, mainly minor mistakes, but occasionally revisions of detail. The fioritura of bar 33, for instance, seems to have been less rhythmically fluid in Chopin's first draft, with the semiquaver groupings continuing into the second half of the bar. The voicing of the left hand (l. h.) at 40 was originally as in 36; the bass note at 45 and 47 was apparently F♯; and the phrasing at 69 had longer spans. Pedalling, expression marks and dynamics were added later and in close detail, though Chopin neglected to add pedalling for the second theme on its first appearance.

The first French edition (Schlesinger) was prepared from this autograph in July 1836. There are numerous minor differences between the *Stichvorlage* and the first edition, including changes to dynamics (added in bars 25 and 30, removed in bar 238); to phrasing (l. h. at 36 *et seq.*, 45–8 and 55–6); to note values in the inner voices (lengthened in 49, 51 and 111–12); and to expression and tempo marks (an added ritardando at 66 and a tempo at 94; an omitted più vivo at 136 and scherzando at 138). It is very likely that several of these changes represent proof corrections made by Chopin himself, but in some cases they are clearly publisher's errors.

The first German edition (Breitkopf & Härtel, plate no. 5706) was prepared in June 1836. Jan Ekier's stemma for the work suggests that it was based on proofs of the Schlesinger edition, to which Chopin had made further corrections.[13] This is incorrect. Krystyna Kobylańska quotes a Breitkopf letter citing the presence of a manuscript of the ballade then (1878) in their collection.[14] This may have been a copy rather than an autograph, but it indicates that Chopin sent a manuscript (rather than proofs) to Leipzig, as he was to do for most subsequent works. The German edition differs from the French in two major and several minor respects. The major changes are a Lento rather than Largo marking for the introduction and a D rather than E♭ in the chord at bar 7. It should be remembered that Chopin had no control over any editorial changes made (often matters of 'house style') in Leipzig. The D here, repeated in many later editions, was probably the work of the publisher. The first English edition was prepared by Wessel in August 1836, probably from the Schlesinger proofs, and it was published as 'La Favorite'. Chopin almost certainly had no hand in its preparation.

The earliest reference to the Second Ballade is in a letter from Chopin to Julian Fontana, sent from Majorca on 14 December 1838: 'I expect to send you my Preludes and Ballade shortly.'[15] A succession of further references followed until April 1839, mainly concerning the arrangements for publishing the work. Then, in a letter of 8 August 1839, there is a final intriguing reference, 'Send me ... my latest Ballade, because I want to look at a certain point.'[16] There is an autograph without title page, probably completed in February 1839, which served as the *Stichvorlage* for the first French edition.[17] It is one of the most heavily corrected of all Chopin's surviving fair copies, and its layers of creative process were revealed by Saint-Saëns in an early – indeed a pioneering – source study of creative process.[18] Among other things Saint-Saëns showed that there were an additional two notes at the opening, that the melody note at bar 7 was F rather than A, that at one stage an extra two bars were inserted at 83, and that the caesura in the main theme at 88 was originally a bar later and lasted a complete bar. He also demonstrated several stages in the genesis of the figuration at 47 and of the bass passages at 189.

The autograph formed the basis for a copy by Adolf Gutman[19] with the title page in the composer's hand (misspelling the dedicatee 'Schuhmann'). The opus number, incorrectly given as Op. 36, is in another hand. A number of minor errors (additional to those on the autograph) appear in Gutman's copy (mainly concerning phrasing and the omission of expression marks), and there are significant autograph glosses, indicating that Gutman's copy was carefully corrected by Chopin before it went to Leipzig. The most notable of these is the 'scoring' of the last two chords, where the left hand is dropped an octave. Chopin had originally written this in the autograph, but later cancelled it. The higher form appears in the French and English first editions, the lower in the German.

The first French edition was prepared by Troupenas in September 1840 (plate no. T. 925) on the basis of the autograph. Ekier provides evidence that Chopin himself corrected the proofs.[20] He argues moreover (mainly on textual evidence) that the first English edition, prepared by Wessel in 1839 and entitled 'La Gracieuse', was based on these corrected proofs before still further corrections were made for the Troupenas edition. The first German edition was prepared in September 1840 (Breitkopf & Härtel, plate no. 6330) based on the Gutman copy.

Minor disagreements between these sources are copious, especially in the phrasing of the main theme. In Gutman and the German edition, for example, slurs begin at bars 39 and 41. The French edition omits the r.h. phrasing at 64–9, while the German follows Gutman in subdividing the autograph l.h. phrasing of the same passage. The German edition also departs from the autograph phrasing of 83–92 and breaks the phrasing of 112–15. None of the editions retains the autograph phrasing of the tenor melody from 115 onwards. There are autograph glosses on the first French editions in collections by Stirling and Jędrzejewicz, notably crosses which serve to isolate the introduction which – as we know from other sources – Chopin would play by itself.[21]

The A♭ major Ballade (No. 3) was composed in autumn 1841. On 18 October Chopin wrote to Fontana that he would receive the Ballade and the Fantasia (Op. 49) towards the end of the week: 'I cannot give them enough polish.'[22] The original of the autograph *Stichvorlage* has been lost but there is a photograph and a facsimile.[23] There is a title page in Chopin's hand with a dedication (à Mademoiselle Pauline Nouilles),[24] the opus number and the names of both Schlesinger and Breitkopf & Härtel. As usual there are minor revisions, some done at the time of composing, others added later (with a different pen).

The Fontana copy is also not extant, though Ekier suggests that it can be reconstructed on circumstantial and textual evidence. It appears, partly from Chopin's correspondence, that the Fontana copy was the basis of the Schlesinger edition, prepared in November 1841 (plate no. 3486), and that Chopin sent the autograph to Breitkopf (1842, plate no. 6652). Detailed stemmatic analysis for this work is complex and to an extent speculative. Jeffrey Kallberg points out that Chopin had just sold the English rights of Opp. 44–9 to Schlesinger who in turn sold them to Wessel in London during January 1842.[25] There is evidence that Moscheles proof-read and 'corrected' the Fontana copy for Wessel, but Kallberg suggests that Chopin demanded the return of the manuscript before it was set, insisting that the Wessel edition should be based on the Schlesinger proofs which he (Chopin) corrected. As Ekier has pointed out, the Wessel edition repeats the Schlesinger variants. A further copy made by Saint-Saëns is of some importance in that it seems to have derived from the Fontana copy rather than from a published edition.[26] It is by examining textual disagreements between the autograph, the Saint-Saëns copy and the three first editions that Ekier notionally reconstructs the Fontana copy.

Unsurprisingly – given the above stemma – textual variants are considerable and it will be possible to indicate only a few here. The German edition omits slurs at bars 5–8 but adds them at 23–5; the French edition omits mezzo voce for the second theme; the French and English editions have no slurs at 75–7 and omit the autograph pedal at 132–3; there are six important accents at 86–7 in the autograph and German edition but not in the French and English editions; there is a major textual difference at 132 (the French edition has l.h. F as against the German edition's chord F–A♭–B♭); there is substantial variation in the l.h. phrasing of the final page. There are also autograph glosses in the collections of Jędrzejewicz and Stirling, notably the inclusion of pedalling for the beginning of second group, bars 49–53. Significantly Chopin added in autograph on the Stirling score 'C'est moi qui ai corrigé toutes ces notes'. There are crosses in the Scherbatoff and Jędrzejewicz scores outlining the end of sections and fingering annotations (possibly autograph) in the Franchomme copy.

On 15 December 1842 Chopin wrote to Breitkopf from Paris offering 'a Scherzo for 600 francs, a Ballade for 600 francs and a Polonaise for 500

Example 7. Rejected autograph of Fourth Ballade. Extracts

francs'.[27] The Ballade in question was No. 4. There is an incomplete autograph for the work in 6/4 rather than 6/8,[28] presumably abandoned because Chopin decided to change the time-signature. Kallberg points out[29] that the inscription 'p[our] Mr. Dessauer' at the top of the first page is not in Chopin's hand (as reported in Kobylańska and Ekier). Rather it was written by Auguste Franchomme who distributed some of Chopin's manuscripts after his death. Ekier's reasoning about the genesis of the Fourth Ballade coinciding with Dessauer's visits to Paris in 1841 is therefore flawed.[30] The rejected autograph contains numerous corrections and variants, some of them very intriguing. The quaver figure in the third bar of the first theme, for instance, was originally as in Ex. 7 (i) on each appearance, with the lower auxiliary cancelled throughout; the r.h. at 38 was originally as Ex. 7 (ii) and 53–4 was as Ex. 7 (iii).

Ekier's proposed stemmas for this Ballade were prepared in apparent ignorance of another incomplete autograph, which clearly postdates the above manuscript. This is the only surviving fair copy of the three which Chopin prepared as *Stichvorlagen* (a letter to Wessel indicates an autograph for the English edition), and it was probably the one sent to Leipzig. It was owned by Mendelssohn's wife and was given to the Bodleian Library, Oxford as part of the Margaret Deneke collection. There is internal evidence that the first German edition was based on this autograph (missing dynamics at the opening, missing slurs at bar 38, placing of the *rit.* at 69 etc.), though the autograph layout of the introduction is followed (at least partly) in the French and not in the German edition, where it is 'rationalised'. This mixed derivation may well support Ekier's hypothesis that the Breitkopf autograph drew upon the other two and was therefore the last to be written.

Editions

The ballades were published in later editions by Brandus (No. 1), Troupenas (No. 2) and Breitkopf & Härtel (Nos. 1, 2 and 3), using the same plate numbers as the original editions but in some cases with revised texts. The three main publishers also brought out collected editions of Chopin's music after his death – Ashdown & Parry (successors to Wessel) in 1860–82, Brandus (who incorporated Schlesinger) in 1859–78 and Breitkopf in 1878–80. The Breitkopf is of special interest as part of a major project of complete editions of mainly German composers. It was prepared by a six-man editorial committee, including Liszt and Brahms, from original manuscripts and the first German edition (though it restores E♭ in the G minor Ballade) and it has become familiar to later students as the basis of the Lea Pocket Scores edition (New York, 1955–62).

Other collected editions began at an early stage, often with the direct involvement of Chopin's pupils, and some at least included the music published posthumously (Meissonier, Paris; Adolf Martin Schlesinger, Berlin) by Julian Fontana in 1855 and 1859 in close consultation with the composer's family. The earliest were the two French editions of 1860, one (Schonenberger) edited by Fétis and the other (Richault) by Chopin's Norwegian pupil Thomas Tellefsen. Already there were significant differences of orientation in these two early editions, although both were based on the same source – the first French editions. Where the Schonenberger set out to achieve a satisfactory text in the judgement of the editor, the Richault tried to recreate the composer's intentions. By modern standards the results are wayward in both cases, but for very different reasons.

In the Schonenberger, departures from autograph and printed sources result from a combination of careless mistakes and what would today be regarded

Example 8. Schonenberger edition: Third Ballade bars 1–8

as over-editing. We may take as an example the two themes of the Third Ballade. The character of the first is entirely compromised by Fétis's phrasing (Ex. 8), textual inaccuracy and the omission of Chopin's dynamics indication; that of the second theme by the omission of mezzo voce, missing ties (71–3, 88–92), an alternative phrasing (l. h. 72; r. h. 73–7), missing accents and a textual inaccuracy (D rather than C in bar 101).

In the Richault, problems arise rather from an attempt to recapture Chopin's performing and teaching methods, relying not only on the annotated first editions of Jane Stirling but on the editor's memories of versions played by Chopin and by his pupils. The ballades are less problematic than some pieces, but even there Tellefsen compounds Schlesinger's errors with his own in several ways. The first theme of No. 1 will serve. We may note that, although based on the French first edition, the chord at bar 7 has a D; the l. h. slur at 27–8 does not extend to the G; slurs are omitted in the r. h. (37–9) and l. h. (43); at 45–6 and 47–8 the slur does not extend to the D; the phrasing of 54–6 follows the first French edition by breaking halfway through 56; and the r. h. note at the beginning of 45 and 47 is F♯ rather than F.

The very different editorial philosophies underlying Schonenberger and Richault continue to inform later nineteenth- and early twentieth-century editions. Tending towards the first approach are two heavily edited Russian editions, one (Stellowsky) of 1861, whose phrasing in particular bears little relation to Chopin's, and the other (Jurgenson) of 1873–6. This latter, edited

Example 9. Kistner edition: Second Ballade bars 104–8

(heavily, and with liberal additions to Chopin's expression and tempo markings) by the Liszt pupil Karl Klindworth, was well travelled and much used. It was later reprinted by Bote & Bock (Berlin, 1880–5) and is best known today as the 'Augener' edition (London, 1879), with further revisions by Xaver Scharwenka in a reissue of 1910. Also in this category are the Köhler edition for Litolff (Brunswick, 1880–5), the Biehl edition for Bosworth (Leipzig, 1892–7) and the Bowerman edition (London, 1892). In all, the changes to dynamics, pedalling, phrasing, expression marks and even fingerings found in manuscript and early printed sources proceed from the assumption that the original texts may be improved upon – 'perfectionnées', as Saint-Saëns remarked caustically.[31] Or, as Ganche put it with no less irony, 'a reviser would be no reviser if he did not revise'.[32] As a result these editions are a valuable source for students of late nineteenth- and early twentieth-century performance practice, particularly in relation to the demands of the late nineteenth-century instrument.

Among the editions which tried to maintain a living link with Chopin were Gebethner & Wolff of Warsaw (1863), authorised by the composer's family and based on German first editions, and Heugel of Paris (1867), edited by Marmontel and based on French first editions. Of special significance was the Kistner edition (Leipzig, 1879) produced by the Chopin pupil Karl Mikuli based on annotated French and German first editions supplemented by copious notes which he made at his own lessons and those of other pupils, and supplied with helpful introductions. This edition was later reprinted by Bessel (Moscow, 1889) and Schirmer (New York, 1949). Although it has frequently been criticised, there are distinguished pianists today who continue to use Mikuli's text in preference to more recent editions. Certainly its documentary importance is unchallenged, but there are many problems with the text, as a brief commentary on the Second Ballade will illustrate. Mikuli's phrasing of

Example 10. Autograph manuscript of Fourth Ballade bars 1–3

the first theme breaks not only at bars 6 and 30 (defensible in the light of Chopin's autograph), but also at 21; the phrasing of the l. h. breaks on the first note of 38 and again in parallel passages; Chopin's slurs are constantly broken between 40 and 46; there is no phrasing of 64–9 and no *ff* marking at 69; the pedal is released too soon throughout 71–4 (a response no doubt to the needs of the late nineteenth-century piano); and the phrasing of bars 90–102 is eccentric to say the least (Ex. 9).

Mikuli's reliance on Chopin's glosses on first editions is also found in the Peters edition (Leipzig, 1879), compiled by Hermann Scholtz using autographs and the annotated printed editions belonging to the Chopin pupils Mlle R. de Konneritz and Georges Mathias. And the whole approach is spelt out clearly in the subtitle of an edition prepared by Jan Kleczyński for Gebethner and Wolff (Warsaw, 1882). Kleczyński refers specifically to 'variants supplied both by the author himself and as passed on by his most celebrated pupils'. Again the results are often problematic, as a consideration of Kleczyński's text for the Fourth Ballade illustrates. Curiously he adopts the (now common) layout of the introduction found in the first German edition rather than that of the autograph (Ex. 10), just as he conforms to the German octave doubling at bar 104, absent in the French edition. But his pedal marks for the introduction have no such source justification and the subsequent text is riddled with curious readings of Chopin's originals. Kleczyński omits the articulation marks at 46 and parallel places, and also the ritenuto at 70; he gives B♮ instead of B♭ and E♮ instead of D♭ in 73; he omits the tie at 85–6 and the accent at 113; he breaks the l. h. phrase at 122 halfway through the bar, beginning a new phrase on the B♭.

There are numerous additional variants in the later stages of Kleczyński's text which disqualify it on any 'objective' scholarly grounds. Yet precisely because of his point of contact with Chopin's pupils, his edition, like those of Tellefsen, Mikuli and Scholtz, has considerable documentary value. As Zofia Chechlińska put it, these texts 'are to a certain extent an expression of the editors' personal reaction to a living Chopin tradition'.[33]

Arguably this approach reached its culminating point in the celebrated edition by Eduard Ganche, known as the Oxford Original Edition (London, 1932) and based almost entirely on the seven-volume annotated collection of Jane Stirling passed on to Ganche by Stirling's niece Anne D. Houston. But a more scholarly rationale might well be offered for Ganche's endeavour. The Stirling scores have special significance as a complete corpus of music (including posthumous publications) and one almost certainly compiled and corrected under Chopin's direct supervision. Since it is probable that he intended these scores to form the basis of a collected edition which might supersede the first French editions, they have arguably a special authority,[34] and this is supported by Chopin's participation in the final index of incipits. The status of the Stirling scores in relation to an authentic edition will no doubt remain controversial, but an edition which was faithful to them would certainly have great merit. Since the Stirling originals have become available it is now clear that the Oxford Original Edition did them very much less than full justice. Not all the variants appear, and of those which are included, not all are correct.

Other early twentieth-century collected editions include Pugno for Universal Edition (Vienna, 1901), Friedman for Breitkopf & Härtel (Leipzig, 1913), Sauer for Schott (Mainz, 1917–20), Brugnoli for Ricordi (Milan, 1923–37) and Cortot for Salabert (Paris, 1941–7), the latter including detailed commentaries, instructions and exercises. There is also a broadly faithful edition prepared by Debussy for Durand (Paris, 1915–16).[35] Unlike many ninteenth-century editions, most of these (Pugno, Brugnoli, Cortot, Debussy) include no variants in the main text, working from the assumption that the edition should be based exclusively on the composer's final version, as far as this can be identified. And the same is true of an even more ambitious scholarly edition which appeared in Poland following World War II (Warsaw, 1949–61). Ostensibly based on the editorial work of Ignacy Paderewski, Ludwig Bronarski and Josef Turczyński, it was produced in the main by Bronarski (Paderewski died before the project was properly under way). The Polish complete edition was in many ways a pioneering venture, referring to the widest possible range of manuscript and printed sources in an attempt to produce a 'definitive' text. While it remains to this day an enormously popular edition, its realisation was deeply flawed. Among other things, Bronarski's practice was to select freely from different sources, arriving at a 'new' version which permissively conflates material from autographs, copies (some of which were mistaken for auto-graphs) and all three first editions. In many cases orthography and phrasing are based not on any legitimate source but on unidentified recent editions and even occasionally on personal judgements made in the light of particular harmonic theories.[36]

Of the other so-called 'source' editions which have been produced in recent years (Henle Verlag, Wiener Urtext and Polish National), the only one as yet nearing completion is the Henle Verlag, edited mainly by Ewald Zimmerman (Duisburg, 1956–) and accompanied by a detailed commentary. Again this is flawed, despite its declared intention to work from a uniform basis of sources, to select a 'best' source and to adhere to it. As Zofia Chechlińska points out, there are in practice numerous importations from other versions and also many inaccuracies.[37] A single example from the ballades will suffice. The phrasing in bars 44–6 of the First Ballade finds no correspondence in either the autograph or the first editions, despite the claims of Zimmerman's commentary.

After many years of gestation the Polish National Edition (Warsaw, 1967–), under Jan Ekier, seems at last to be making some headway, albeit only by sacrificing (or delaying) for subsequent volumes the remarkably detailed commentaries which accompanied the first volume, the ballades. This does indeed look set to become the standard Chopin. Inevitably it has its shortcomings, as the commentary to the ballades illustrates. Ekier's stemmatic analyses, ingenious though their reasoning often appears, are at times inaccurate or incomplete and this resonates into later editorial choices. Nor can its elaborately scientific commentary conceal a subjective element in the selection of variants between, for example, autographs and first editions, given the frequent uncertainties about Chopin's participation in the correction of proofs. Ekier's claim to give 'the most thorough presentation of the authentic, unadulterated musical text of Chopin's works as the composer intended it' still hinges by and large on the privilege of final thoughts (by no means axiomatic in the editing of Chopin's music). At the same time he recognises that to identify a single 'final text' in Chopin is not always possible, and his incorporation of variants is an explicit acknowledgement that one should rather speak of 'final texts'.

In reality there can be no edition of Chopin which will be satisfactory in every respect, given the complexity of the manuscript tradition. The point has been well made by Chechlińska, Higgins, Eigeldinger and others. Indeed it has been persuasively argued[38] that the many variants in Chopin's music are a part of its aesthetic property, and that an adequate recognition of the contemporary

Example 11. Hugo Riemann edition Second Ballade bars 1–6

social status of his manuscripts would render questionable any of the usual laws of first or final intentions. For all that, editions need to be made, and there must be clear criteria for their preparation. The Polish National Edition of the ballades may have its inadequacies, but it can be recommended to performers on two important counts. First it is an edition based largely on a single ('best') source which is clearly identified, rather than a conflation of several sources. This is by no means always an infallible *modus*, but it is by far the most sensible approach to Chopin editing. And secondly it indicates, in an admirably detailed separate commentary, the most important existing variants, enabling the performer (rather than the editor) to make a conflation where appropriate.

There are of course countless 'performing' (as opposed to scholarly) editions of the ballades. Some are directly pedagogical in intention. Of these the most remarkable are Hugo Riemann's 'phrased editions' of Op. 38 and Op. 47 (Leipzig, 1886–91), which are *de facto* analyses, using numbers below the barline and various 'reading signs' to outline the main components of the form. Ex. 11 illustrates Riemann's analysis of Op. 38, significantly described as 'in A minor'. Others include the Holmes and Karn edition in 'The Academic Series' (London, 1893) and Frank Merrick's (Novello) *Chopin edition for students* (London, 1935–53), which includes editorial pedalling, fingering and metronome markings.

Other performing editions are aimed at a more popular market, even involving simplification of Chopin's text, as in King Palmer's arrangement of 'The Famous Ballade in G minor' (London, 1947). And more remote still from Chopin are the many transcriptions of various kinds which remained popular well into the twentieth century. They include four-hand arrangements of all four ballades, arrangements for violin and piano of the first two, and arrangements of Op. 38 for organ, for cello and piano (Franchomme) and for voice and piano ('A Barcarolle at Dawn' to words by H. Bellamy; 'La Fille d'onde' to words by E. Richebourg). There is even an accordion arrangement of Op. 47. In such transcriptions the music naturally takes on a quite new meaning. And in that respect they are a dimension of broader aspects of reception.

Critics

Nineteenth-century critical writing – books, articles and reviews – does not extend our knowledge of Chopin reception very far beyond professional musical circles. It cannot tell us much about the reception of his music by audiences and amateur performers, except to the extent that criticism may help shape attitudes and form opinions, however indirectly. During his lifetime Chopin was of course his own advocate, and among a small constituency of initiates (especially in Paris) he gained an almost legendary reputation. His public concerts were few, however, and as a result his appearances as a performer were less widely reported in the press than those of other pianist-composers.[39] Relatively few reviews of the ballades flowed from such appearances, though there are generous accounts of the second and third following major concerts in Paris, London and Edinburgh.[40] In general, reviews of his music were more often consequent on publication than on performance. And since the music was published simultaneously in France, Germany and England, the critical debate ranged widely and source material is plentiful.

Already during his lifetime Chopin's music was taken up by other pianists and its popularity increased steadily throughout the century. Yet despite the claim that by the end of the century there was 'hardly a concert programme without his name',[41] it was a rather selective repertory which was played, above all the simpler dance pieces and a handful of nocturnes and preludes. Of larger works, the concertos found a place in orchestral programmes, but the sonatas, scherzos, ballades and fantasies (Op. 49 and Op. 61) were much less frequently given, even by professional pianists. These works were victims of a widely-held nineteenth-century view of Chopin: that 'while great in small things he was small ... in great ones',[42] that he was 'incapable of continuous effort'.[43] Repertory studies suggest, indeed, that the ballades were among the least featured genres in the nineteenth century, though within this limitation some were favoured more than others.[44] It seems that – shortly after its publication in Paris – the Second Ballade was for a time much *en vogue*.[45] But the more enduring favourites were the first and third, which by the end of the century were fast becoming 'hopelessly vulgarised'.[46] The fourth, on the other hand, retained its reputation for technical difficulty and inaccessibility well into our present century.[47]

Needless to say critical writing on the ballades did not initially detail technical issues, except to express bewilderment, especially at their novelty of form.[48] The nineteenth-century critic was less interested in formulating theories than in conveying his experience of a work directly to his readers, and the metaphor was his principal tool. In the case of the ballades the temptation was to allow the genre title to make even more specific the customary references to non-musical designates. Schumann set the ball rolling with his remarks about Mickiewicz. In due course references to specific poetic ballads (entirely without documentary validation) were sufficiently congealed to enable Huneker, Cortot and even Bourniquel to cite them as though they had unquestioned authority. The tradition is least stable with the first and last ballades, whose reputed links with *Konrad Wallenrod* (not itself a ballad) and *Trzech budrysów* respectively were never presented in any but the most generalised terms.

For the second and third ballades the associations with Mickiewicz were more specific. Yet there is considerable confusion about this. The poems *Świteź* and *Świtezianka* have both been assigned to No. 2 at various times, while No. 3 has been related to *Undine*, although there is no such poem by Mickiewicz.[49] The most coherent associations are between No. 2 and *Świteź* (see pp. 16–17) and between No. 3 and *Świtezianka*, since the latter is indeed the tale of an 'undine', in effect a version of the familiar *Rusalka* legend. The opening of No. 3 has been depicted as a dialogue between the two lovers by the lake (treble and tenor registers), while the ending 'vividly depicts the ultimate drowning in some abyss, of the fated youth'.[50]

Such links with Mickiewicz were a commonplace of nineteenth-century criticism and they inevitably encouraged a national perspective on the ballades, especially – it need hardly be added – in Poland, where Chopin was often viewed as a powerful symbol of national identity. Deferring only to the mazurkas and polonaises, the ballades were held to be among Chopin's most 'Polish' works, with the second in particular described in some quarters as the 'Polish ballade'.[51] Nor was this tendency confined to Poland. One British reviewer remarked in 1848 that 'the concluding piece was also national, the ballade'.[52] The comment is significant, since the intriguing network of associations on which it is based is deemed to require no word of explication.

Even where specific literary programmes were not invoked – 'each sees in the music [of No. 1], as in the clouds, different things'[53] – the tradition of viewing the ballades as wordless narratives persisted. 'The first eight bars [of No. 3] are, as it were, the introduction to some "story".'[54] The opening of No. 1 is 'Listen, I will tell you how it happened.'[55] Kleczyński refers to 'veritable dramatic recitations',[56] while Ehlert claims that 'Chopin narrates a story, but one which has never taken place, except as an odyssey of the spirit.'[57] Karasowski summarises the position, remarking that some 'called them "poetical stories". Indeed there is about them a certain narrative character which is particularly well rendered by the 6/8 and 6/4 time and which makes them differ essentially from the traditional forms.'[58]

For many critics the poetic quality of the ballades was more a matter of 'feeling' than of 'narrative'. 'We may as well introduce at once the grand cry of the day; it is *Feeling*.'[59] It was above all in France that Chopin the 'romantic composer' – the 'poet' of the piano who expressed the depths of his inner world to all of us – was cultivated. 'To listen to Chopin is to read a strophe by Lamartine';[60] 'Chopin is *par excellence* a pianist of the emotions';[61] '[he] is above all a poet, a sensitive poet who places poetry at the forefront of everything';[62] through music he 'reveals his suffering';[63] the music of the First Ballade 'tells of a mysterious sadness; we fall into a deep reverie'.[64] The image of Chopin as a composer of deep feeling ('melancholy' and 'morbidity' were favoured terms) suited the purposes of the major journal in Paris, Schlesinger's *Gazette musicale de Paris* (later the *Revue et Gazette musicale de Paris*). The *Gazette* championed Chopin at the expense of more shallow virtuoso composers, and (in at least some reviews) these were deemed to include Liszt. Even Maurice Bourges, by no means always a friend to Chopin's music, wrote in the *Gazette* of the Third Ballade: 'Here we find him giving vent to his unfettered imagination in an unusually grandiose way. An invigorating warmth, a rare vitality permeate the happy succession of phrases, as harmonious as they are melodious. It is poetry in translation, but a superior translation made through sounds alone.'[65]

It would clearly be over-schematic to characterise Chopin reception rigidly in national terms. Yet intriguing generalisations do emerge from a study of the critics. If the ballades were songs of the homeland in Poland and poetic effusions in France, they were often 'music of intellect' in Germany and England – 'advanced', aloof, even iconoclastic in character. There were of course conflicting views about the value of such modernist tendencies. During his lifetime (from 1833) Chopin was well served in this regard by the *Allgemeine musikalische Zeitung* and by Schumann's *Neue Zeitschrift für Musik*, but attacked (at least until 1839) by Rellstab's *Iris*. In England there was a similar division, with *The Musical Standard* and *The Athenaeum* (Henry Chorley) broadly favourable, and *The Musical World* (J. W. Davison) antagonistic.

There are striking parallels in the rhetoric. Schumann described Op. 23 as 'one of Chopin's wildest and most original compositions' and Op. 38 as 'equally imaginative and intellectually ingenious [*geistreich*]'. The composer of the Third Ballade was 'the cultured, intellectual Pole'.[66] Compare the references in England. His was a 'music of intellect'; there is 'a complete absence of the commonplace';[67] 'he could no more put down a commonplace than could Milton a platitude or Bacon a paradox';[68] like Berlioz he will 'never descend to flatter popular taste'.[69] And the notion of an élitist, avant-garde art – a 'mysterious language which belongs only to himself'[70] – was fostered especially of the ballades: 'Chopin has rarely advanced his peculiar system of harmony further than in this [third] ballade.'[71]

By the same token Rellstab's reference to 'ear-splitting discords, forced transitions, harsh modulations, ugly distortions of melody and rhythm'[72] found their echo in England with criticism of the 'needlessly crude and hazardous modulations', the 'crude and conceited turns which Chopin can rarely resist introducing'[73] and – in Davison's diatribe in *The Musical World* – the 'motley surface of ranting hyperbole and excruciating cacophony' which characterises 'the entire works of Chopin'.[74] Even Rellstab's conversion to Chopin was paralleled in a way by Davison's admittedly ambivalent change of position in *An Essay on the Works of Frederick Chopin*.[75]

It is notable that as Chopin's popularity widened in Germany in the later nineteenth century, views about him polarised in yet another direction – less a divided opinion about the merits of his modernism than a more fundamental division between Chopin as modernist and Chopin as salon composer. Adherents to the former view included some of the most progressive critics and composers of the day, including Brahms, Wagner, von Bülow and the Liszt circle, for whom the ballades were true 'symphonic poems'. Yet despite the advocacy of such figures Chopin was increasingly absorbed into the repertory of domestic *Trivialmusik* in Germany, and at least some works (unlike most of Liszt's) proved marketable in these terms. The dissemination of his music always owed more to the publisher than to the professional pianist. Yet it is by no means clear that the major extended works were widely taken up by amateur pianists in the days before recordings brought them into our living-rooms. The claim (at the end of the century) that Chopin had become 'the property of every schoolgirl'[76] needs substantial qualification, not only as to social groups and regions but also as to genres. Given the technical (not to say musical) difficulties posed by his major works, we might reasonably assume that it was the waltzes, mazurkas, preludes and early nocturnes which dominated the domestic repertory, and that the constituency for the ballades among amateur musicians in the nineteenth century was by no means great.

One critic complained of the 'impossibilities which Chopin ... imposes upon the amateur player'.[77]

The force-field between an avant-garde and *Trivialmusik* in Chopin reception speaks eloquently of German culture in the second half of the nineteenth century. And it is intriguing to find both poles separated out, as it were, in Russia and England during the same period. Where Russia stressed Chopin's modernism, not only through critical writing but through his influence on a substantial corpus of Russian music from Balakirev onwards, England rather lost sight of this quality (much noted in the early part of the century) in favour of a wholesale domestication of his music. The extended pieces were treated with suspicion ('Icarus has flown too near the sun, and the borrowed wings have no longer the strength to support him')[78] and 'a certain drawing-room atmosphere'[79] was emphasised. Chopin pieces became 'tuneful gems' and 'pearls', little distinguished from the ephemeral drawing-room music surrounding them. Here, as elsewhere in the nineteenth century, particular groups of listeners heard in the music what they needed to hear.

Our own century adopted yet another perspective. Already in monographs by Niecks and Scharlitt[80] there was a studied attempt to recover Chopin from the salon for English and German readers respectively. And this in turn encouraged a fresh evaluation of his extended works, not least the ballades, which emerged from the periphery into the centre-stage of Chopin reception. Above all, their literary and programmatic associations were played down in favour of their purely musical values, and in particular the strength and stability of their structures. As George Bernard Shaw put it, 'Chopin's ballades are no more programme music than the slow movement of a Mozart concerto.'[81]

There was in reality a subtle but all-pervasive shift in the nature of aesthetic understanding in the early years of our century. Increasingly the tendency was to de-contextualise the musical work, to let it make its own statement, to assign it a monadic character whose meaning might be revealed only through analysis, itself a discipline of our age, and one whose aims were by no means congruent with those of nineteenth-century criticism. Germany paved the way for an analytical appreciation of the ballades, first through the work of Hugo Riemann and later in a major study by his disciple Hugo Leichtentritt.[82] But it was above all the adoption of Chopin by Heinrich Schenker which set the compass reading for a wealth of later analytical research, notably in Anglo-American scholarship since World War II.

Some of this research will be invoked in due course. But it should be noted here that the shift in aesthetic has been no less manifest in performance styles.

There has been an almost neo-classical attempt to purge Chopin playing of late-romantic excesses and to 'recover' aspects of contemporary performance practice, even down to the use of period instruments. At the same time there have been fresh thoughts about repertory, and in particular a leaning towards major extended structures such as the ballades – precisely those works which fared least well in the nineteenth century. Even the manner of programming such works changed significantly in our century. It is a far cry from Chopin's practice of performing just the opening section of No. 2 to the present (implicitly structuralist) tendency to perform all four ballades as a cycle.[83] The 'wordless narratives' of Chopin's age have become today's 'triumphs of architecture'.

Pianists

In other respects too we may well wonder what Chopin would make of present-day performances of the ballades. He would of course be struck by the greater weight and volume of the post-1850 instrument, by its uniformity of tone colour and by attendant changes in the nature and function of the pedal. And while he might concede the gains, he would surely feel acutely the loss of delicacy (especially in the bass) and of tonal differentiation between the registers. Other changes are perhaps more subtle, dependent on aspects of early nineteenth-century performance practice that cannot be recovered with precision. There is evidence that Chopin's own tempos in performance, especially in lyrical, cantabile sections, were faster and more fluent than is usual today.[84] Equally it would seem that some of his expression marks carried a meaning that is no longer associated with them. Jan Ekier has suggested, for instance, that Chopin's legato sometimes referred to the classical practice of sustaining harmony notes rather than linking melody notes. Even the vexed question of his rubato needs to be viewed within an historical context.[85]

There are many verbal descriptions of Chopin's playing, and it goes without saying that they are less than adequate to its reliable evocation.[86] Yet it is clear from such descriptions (by critics and pupils) that his discriminating sensitivity of touch, carefully shaded dynamics, intricate pedal effects and discreet rubato added up to an utterly unique pianism, drawing upon and perhaps synthesising aspects of Hummel's 'brilliant' manner[87] and of Field's lyricism, but in the end quite unlike either. His letters and abortive pedagogical notes further establish that his approach to technique – especially fingering and pedalling – was anything but orthodox. Chopin playing Chopin was in short quite different from anyone else playing Chopin. And that included Liszt's overtly expressive and flamboyant interpretations as well as the more restrained and studied – even intellectual – readings of Clara Schumann and Hans von Bülow, so far as these can be re-created from contemporary accounts.[88] As we enter the second half of the century we move yet further from Chopin's own classically rooted playing. Again the data are inadequate, but when we add to verbal descriptions the evidence of the editions (many of them made by leading Chopin exponents) it seems clear that the music was increasingly reinterpreted from the standpoint of a late-romantic æsthetic essentially alien from Chopin himself.

Several frameworks have been proposed by commentators in an attempt to reduce the empirical variety of Chopin playing to some semblance of order.[89] One is based on pedagogical traditions, tracing Chopin playing through the composer's pupils and grandpupils and comparing this genealogy with, for example, genealogies of Chopin playing deriving from Liszt and Leschetizky. The most influential Chopin pupils were undoubtedly Mikuli (who taught Michalowski, Rosenthal and Koczalski), and Mathias (who taught Philipp, Pugno and Carreño). The next generation would include Neuhaus, Sofronitsky and Rosen in the Mikuli line; Magaloff and Novaes in the Mathias line. These lines might then be compared with Liszt pupils such as Tausig,[90] Sauer and von Bülow, and above all with Leschetizky pupils, who included Friedman, Paderewski, Moiseiwitsch and Sliwiński. Yet given the range of influences to which any artist is susceptible, not to mention the singular personalities of the great performers, it is difficult to establish any very clear causality in these genealogies.

A second framework considers national schools as a determinant of performing styles. Here too the ground is anything but firm, though some characteristics do emerge. There is a case for identifying certain peculiarly Russian traits, deriving in some measure from the playing and teaching of Anton Rubinstein, who more than anyone accommodated Chopin's music to the concert hall rather than the salon. 'It is clever, but not Chopinesque', commented Hallé. The Polish pianist Józef Hofmann was among Rubinstein's many pupils and elements of a Russian 'school' might also be detected in the playing of Rakhmaninov and the Safonov pupil Joseph Lhevinne. It is also common to identify a French 'Chopin', affected by specific conservatory traditions – the Chopin of Planté, Cortot, Casadesus and Long, and, in a later generation, of Perlemuter and François. Long herself referred to 'gracefulness, elegance, clarity, moderation and suppleness'.[91] But such generalisations grow weaker as the evidence accumulates, and they are undoubtedly an easy prey to wishful thinking.

They can be made a little more concrete with reference to different technical traditions stemming from Lebert-Stark, Deppe, Leschetizky, Breithaupt and Matthay.[92] But even here the tendency is for great performers to transcend categories. The likelihood is that Chopin playing was influenced more by the changing fashions of successive generations than by teacher–pupil relations, nationality or technical 'schools'. In comparing different recordings of the ballades, then, a chronological approach will be adopted. It should be stressed that no more than a sketch is offered and that it makes no pretensions to objectivity.

The earliest recording of a Chopin ballade is a performance of No. 3, recorded in 1912 by Vladimir de Pachmann (1848–1933), second only to Paderewski as a Chopin specialist of the day. Only the second half of the work (from bar 116) has survived, but this emerges nonetheless as an outstanding interpretation. For today's audience the rubato introduces an immediate difficulty, notably in the 'waltz' episode at bar 124 and the reprise of Theme I at bar 213. In both cases Pachmann sacrifices a sense of momentum in the interests of local expression. His rubato extends, moreover, to the relation between larger sections of the work, and this is a feature which has survived into the performance practice of our own time, albeit in less extreme form. The reprise of Theme II (157) is taken at the remarkably fast tempo of $\downarrow$. = 84, for instance. It is interesting to find similar fluctuations of tempo both of detail and larger paragraphing in the piano roll performance by Teresa Carreño (1853–1917). Here the waltz episode employs what can only be described as a 'notes inégales' technique. There is a massive ritardando before the return of Theme II at 146, and – as in Pachmann – a compensatory increase in tempo at 157.

The range of interpretative licence in early twentieth-century performance is evident in the contrast between two recordings of No. 3 dating from 1925, by Rakhmaninov (1873–1943) and the Polish pianist Ignaz Friedman (1882–1948). Rakhmaninov's interpretation is certainly the most remarkable on record, effectively polarising the work into two halves. His exposition is exceptionally slow, so that even the contrasting material at bar 9 is given a mellow, ruminative character (it should be noted that this is one of the few early recordings which do not crescendo through bars 11–12). Theme II fluctuates between $\downarrow$. = 48 and $\downarrow$. = 54, confirming this as a deeply expressive, introverted reading of the main thematic material, no doubt very Russian in character. The second half of the work is then a gradual accelerando through the 'waltz' episode into the reprise of Theme II which positively gallops, with strong half-bar accents, into the development. Rakhmaninov pays no attention to Chopin's smorzando at bar 187, allowing the momentum to continue unchecked through to the reprise of Theme I.

In contrast Friedman – a Leschetizky pupil – offers a brisk, even aggressive, reading of Theme I turning the ♪♩ pattern of bars 9ff into a ♪♩ (martellato), and building not only a massive crescendo through 11–12 but a premature climax towards the end of the section. Nothing could be further removed from Rakhmaninov's deeply expressive performance. Like many other pianists, Friedman changes tempo entirely for Theme II, taking it at ♩. = 78 as opposed to Rakhmaninov's ♩. = 48–54. There is a general air of indiscipline about this performance, although Friedman's technical acumen is not in doubt. The reprise of Theme II, for example, is played at such a speed that the beauties of the left-hand countermelody are totally lost.[93] Equally the tendency to allow very substantial ritardandos at phrase endings (as at 102 and 144–6) is problematical to modern ears, while the ritardando at the beginning of the reprise of Theme I entirely dissipates momentum at a critical stage.

These early recordings bring us close to nineteenth-century traditions in their fluid tempos, their rubato and their frequent disrespect for Chopin's markings. It is hard to know how close to Chopin's original conception they may be, but it seems likely that they bear the imprint rather of a late nineteenth-century æsthetic. It is worth remembering Mikuli's account of Chopin's playing as 'always measured, chaste, distinguished and at times even severely reserved'.[94] One 1920s recording of No. 3 to which Mikuli's description might well be applied is that of Alfred Cortot (1877–1962). Cortot retains a point of contact with nineteenth-century traditions but at the same time evinces a more twentieth-century concern for textual accuracy and structure. A stylish rubato is still very much present, but the eccentricities of tempo are gone (Theme II is now an accommodating ♩. = 63) and the control of pacing and intensity are such that the work makes sense as a whole. This is especially clear in the development. Cortot is the only one of the pianists discussed who succeeds in maintaining intensity here while at the same time registering the (relatively) more relaxed quality of the Theme I references.

All five recordings of No. 3 were made before 1930 and by pianists who were born before 1885. Naturally there is no absolute dividing-line between the old and the middle generations of pianists in our century. Of those born in the later 1880s and 1890s some belong to an older school while others have clearly adopted a more 'modern' performance style. It is interesting, for example, to compare recordings of No. 4 by two Polish pianists born in the 1880s, Raoul Koczalski (1885–1948) and Artur Rubinstein (1887–1982). Admittedly the recordings are separated by twelve years (1938 and 1950 respectively). In several particulars Koczalski, a grandpupil of Chopin through Mikuli, retains a close link with nineteenth-century traditions in his extraordinary performance. The introduction is dispensed with briskly. Theme I is then treated to a constant rubato of a kind which seems mannered to contemporary ears, but which is persuasive for all that. The waltz rhythms are 'pointed' by staccato articulations in the left-hand weak beats, and a major expressive device is the deliberate lack of synchronisation between the two hands. By contrast Rubinstein's introduction is liquid and smooth, effecting a seamless and integral link to Theme I which is in turn restrained in expression and carefully measured in intensity, but which lacks the richness and character imparted to it by Koczalski. Essentially Rubinstein replaces right-hand rubato with rallentando and accelerando.

This contrast is replicated in less extreme form in the recordings by Vladimir Horowitz (1904–89) and Solomon (1902–88). Again Horowitz takes the introduction very fast – a succession of rapid dynamic swells – and again he allows considerable expressive rubato in Theme I, though without Koczalski's mannerism. Solomon, on the other hand, gives a controlled reading of the opening, pacing the repetitions in Theme I to preserve the momentum. We may add to the comparison the recording by the Leschetizky pupil Benno Moiseiwitsch (1890–1963). His interpretation of the introduction is closer to Solomon than to Horowitz, but by increasing the dynamic level of the second phrase he makes it even more strongly anticipative of Theme I. The theme itself is expressive and ruminative in character, but as it progresses Moiseiwitsch departs interestingly from the interpretations of both Horowitz and Solomon, especially in the matter of large-scale rubato. Horowitz and Solomon play the episode at bar 38 very slowly and expressively, picking up speed at 46 (abruptly in Solomon's case). Moiseiwitsch, on the other hand, races off at 38 and slows down at 46, neatly reversing the expressive sequence. There is nothing in the text to tell us one way or the other, and it is intriguing that both readings are convincing and compelling.

The reprise of No. 4 is handled very differently by all four pianists. Solomon allows a gradual, inexorable increase in tension throughout, which leads him to the structural dominant at bar 202, though he then dissipates the tension by playing the chords much slower than written. Horowitz has much more local fluctuation of tempo and dynamics, allowing individual moments of gentleness at the expense of drive and momentum. Intriguingly he pedals right through to the pianissimo chords at 203, whereas Moiseiwitsch actually keeps the pedal right down through the chords so that the dominant pedal in the bass rings through. It is difficult to feel satisfied with many pianists' response to this most critical moment in the work. Rubinstein's performance is also problematic, losing energy by allowing a ritardando before 202. The one recording of this vintage which seems to place the moment perfectly in relation to the structure is by the French pianist Vlado Perlemuter (b. 1904) whose sense of flow and grasp of overall structure seem as infallible as they are effortless.

For a younger generation of pianists (born after 1935) there has been a predictable smoothing out of interpretative differences. Even so individual temperaments remain distinctive, as three readings of No. 1 indicate. Krystian Zimerman (b. 1956) takes both the Introduction and Theme I at an unusually slow pace, investing each moment with interest to the point of fussiness (the staccato articulation at the end of the fioritura at bar 33 is especially mannered). Theme II is then – paradoxically – faster than most readings, but with an elastic phrasing which preserves its expressive quality. Vladimir Ashkenazy (b. 1937) has a more measured 'straight' approach to the entire section, but goes on to treat the figurative material (from 126) as a *tour de force*, adopting speeds which emphasise its lightweight, episodic character. Maurizio Pollini (b. 1942) seems to combine the best of the other two. His introduction is magnificently dramatic and succeeds in effecting a real transformation of mood within a few bars. His Theme I is more expressive than Ashkenazy's but less precious than Zimerman's and his middle section adopts a realistic tempo, avoiding the skittishness of Ashkenazy's interpretation and successfully integrating this section with the rest of the work.

It is clear from these recent recordings that the individual characterisation of material now takes place within a much narrower range of possibilities. Nowhere do we find the rhythmic fluctuations and dynamic contrasts characteristic of the recording of No. 1 by Józef Hofmann (1876–1957), for example, to say nothing of his licence in changing Chopin's note values. Hofmann begins Theme I at an unusually fast tempo (only Casadesus takes it faster in his recording of 1930), but he balances this by allowing substantial ritardandos at bars 27 and 29 (compare Carreño, who almost grinds to a halt between 26 and 32). Hofmann's dynamics are also eccentric, happily ignoring and in some cases (e.g. 99–100) reversing Chopin's markings.

There are, then, perceptible differences of approach between the generations. Yet in the end these remain surface aspects of a performer's response to great music, and I remain dubious of the value of identifying performance traditions too closely even on a period basis. A cross-section of recordings of No. 2 cutting across the generations confirms that the work is recreated in ways which are infinitely variable. There is the richly expressive performance of Koczalski, given a distinctive flavour by the non-synchronisation of hands in the second appearance of Theme I and in the subsequent development section. There is the 'straight' reading of Casadesus, where Theme I is deliberately divested of expression and Theme II (presumably not deliberately) of power. There is the extraordinary interpretation by Sviatoslav Richter (b. 1914), where Theme I is slow, imbued with expressive nuance and rubato at every turn and built to a climax which ignores Chopin's markings and totally compromises the innocence of the melody. Theme II is then rendered in furious anger and taken at such a speed that all the energy of the cross-rhythms is lost (compare Arrau's controlled intensity at this point in a reading which is well aware of the closing section yet to come). There is the cold, brittle virtuosity of Ivo Pogorelich (b. 1958). And there is the carefully graded intensity of Zimerman, who controls the development in such a way that the closing section is given special electricity.

Chopin playing fascinates because of this endless variety. There can be few composers about whom the particularity of different interpretations matters so much to the listener, to the point of performer fetishism in many cases. If there is a ready explanation for this, it lies in Chopin's special sensitivity to the limitations and potentialities of the instrument itself. Since the music draws its substance so very directly from the nature of the piano, the recreation of that substance makes special demands on the performer and elicits special responses from the listener. In the end, of course, the music survives because it is larger than all its possible interpretations. Of their nature particular readings of the ballades isolate some features at the expense of others. Yet the musical texts are infinitely richer than any such isolation of their individual qualities can possibly yield, and it is to the texts that we now turn.

3

Form and design

Ballade No. 1, Op. 23

A structuralist ideal has often guided music analysis, especially in its formative stages as an independent discipline. Implicit in a good deal of analysis has been the notion that structure is stable, and that it may be located in terms inherent in the work itself, unpolluted by context. This is a chimera, since analytical tools are themselves historical categories which have acquired the status of conventions. Yet the notion has somehow remained seductive. We are told by one commentator on the ballades that 'it would be foolish to regard these pieces from the point of view of sonata movements'; and that in any case 'the student should examine every sonata movement as though it were the first example of its kind he has ever seen'.[1] In its way this approach is just as unhelpful as a prescriptive identification of the musical work with an abstract schema. Both positions ignore the true value of compositional norms (to both composer and listener) as one pole of a vital creative dialectic between universal and particular, collective and unique, schema and deviation. A revealing analysis is in this sense always comparative.

Far from ignoring sonata form we need to recognise it as the essential reference point for all four ballades – the 'ideal type' or archetype against which unique statements have been counterpointed. Other formal archetypes, notably rondo and variation form, may be invoked in particular cases, but these remain of subsidiary significance. Indeed it has already been suggested that an important motivation for the ballades was the accommodation of sonata-based structures to an idiom derived from post-classical concert repertories. An analysis which does not invoke sonata form will miss much of the force-field which exists in this music between the exemplifying and the unique.

In the G minor Ballade elements of sonata form are already an obvious background to the presentation of the main thematic groups. The exposition may be outlined schematically as in Figure 1, using text-book terminology. It need scarcely be added that the representation of tonal process in such diagrams is crude.

	Bars	Tonality
Introduction	1–7	
Theme I	8–44	G minor
Transition	44–67	
Theme II	67–93	E♭ major

Figure 1

Tonal relations here deviate from classical practice, but at the same time they depend upon an awareness of that practice. The introduction is a recitative, composing out a Neapolitan harmony in preparation for Theme I (Ex. 2i) in the tonic key of G minor. As Theme II (Ex. 2ii) approaches, Chopin prepares the expected key of B♭ major through its dominant in the classical manner and thwarts this only at the last moment by adding the seventh which directs the music towards E♭ major. Initially VI appears therefore in the character of a 'substitute' for III.

In the reprise Chopin deviates more radically from classical functions (Figure 2).

	Bars	Tonality
Theme II	166–93	E♭ major
Theme I	194–207	(G minor)
Closing section (Theme IV)	208–64	G minor

Figure 2

By presenting a mirror reprise and retaining the same tonal setting as in the exposition for the two themes he establishes an element of symmetry, both thematically and tonally. This is an important dimension of the work's structure. Yet other factors run counter to it. Theme II is now transformed into an impassioned fortissimo statement and Theme I is presented not in its stable exposition form but in the tension-generating form which opened the development section. Here the theme was stated over a dominant pedal and its falling major second was inverted. Figure 3 indicates synoptically these two complementary readings of thematic process.

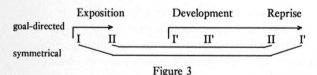

Figure 3

The development section further reinterprets classical function, and in a manner which helps to focus Chopin's specifically dramatic or 'narrative' view of the ballade as a genre. Much of the interest in the work lies in the destiny of the two principal thematic ideas or characters, their variation, transformation and mutual interaction. The development brings them into direct collision, with transitional material omitted, and the continuity between them is all the greater since they share a single tonality of A minor/A major, at least on the most immediate 'foreground' level of tonal organisation. This in turn strengthens their motivic association. The point of contact between them is the more expressive in that Theme I strives heroically to reach the high B with which Theme II starts and almost fails to make it. The later stages of both themes are transformed in this development section to allow the one to grow naturally out of the other and to maintain a single sweep of tension-building material which reaches its climax at bars 124–6.

At this point there is a major structural downbeat, as an extended dominant harmony signals the return of E♭ major, and thematic material gives way to figuration. The dominant harmony is composed out through octatonic figuration (alternating tones and semitones) of a kind not uncommon in Chopin.[2] The regained VI (bar 138) is then celebrated by a fully characterised waltz episode (Theme III), whose phraseology is unmistakably the moto perpetuo arabesque so often found in the independent waltzes, as Ex. 1 has already demonstrated. The main events of the development section might be summarised then as in Figure 4.

	Bars	Tonality
Theme I'	94–105	(A minor)
Theme II'	106–25	(A major)
Transition	126–37	
Theme III	138–65	E♭ major

Figure 4

And, since the waltz appears after all the thematic material has been presented, it functions as a pivot between statement and reprise, once more encouraging a symmetrical interpretation of the work's thematic process, where the waltz would form the peak of an extended thematic arch. This is emphasised by the whole-tone steps underlying the figuration which follows Theme III (bars 150–4) matching the octatonic figuration which precedes it. The foreground tonalities may also be presented as a symmetry, though it is not congruent with the thematic symmetry (Figure 5).

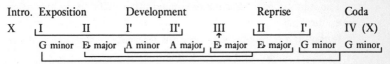

Figure 5

47

Example 12. Schenker analysis of First Ballade (*Free Composition* Vol. 2 No. 153)

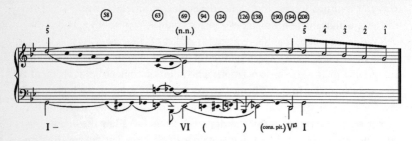

Again it must be stressed that the arch-like character of the work's formal and tonal organisation is counterpointed against a strongly directional momentum more in the spirit of the sonata-form archetype. And in this latter reading the A minor/major tonality is recognised as unstable, taken in as part of a lengthy prolongation of a neighbour note at bar 69. This language immediately invokes the great Austrian theorist Heinrich Schenker, whose analysis of the Ballade, presented as an harmonic reduction or 'graph', is characteristically impressive and perceptive.[3] Schenker indicates a single span between the E♭ major of Theme II in the exposition and the 'regaining' of that tonality with the waltz theme (Ex. 12). He also helpfully differentiates in harmonic terms between Theme I' as presented at the opening of the development section and later in the reprise. In the former the dominant pedal (in A minor, bar 94) functions contrapuntally, while in the latter it has a structural harmonic role, preparing the G minor affirmation of the closing section.

Schenker's directional view of the structure is strengthened by a consideration of the intensity curve of the work as a whole. This builds through the development section to a major pinnacle at bar 124, subsides again with the waltz, rebuilds to a subsidiary peak with the reprise of II and reaches its maximum intensity point with the cumulative closing section.[4] Here, as so often in Chopin, virtuosity has a cathartic function, resolving earlier tensions. And this is enhanced by the change of metre and by the absence of an obvious thematic link with the main body of the work, though the falling second of the main theme cuts through the figuration and contributes to the tragic (rather than merely 'brilliant') character of the final peroration, as Anatoly Leikin has noted.[5] The tragic note is deepened by the dramatic return of a recitative idiom in the final bars, and the interruptive quality here intensifies, if anything, the final violent drive to the cadence. Yet it is characteristic of the Ballade that in a purely formal sense this reference to a recitative idiom acts as a necessary completion of the thematic arch.

Example 13. First Ballade reduction bars 1–9

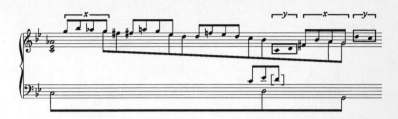

There is, then, a calculated ambiguity in the formal design of the Ballade between a sonata-based structure, allied to an accelerating intensity curve, and the more closed formal symmetry of an arch design. Something of this ambiguity is also reflected in smaller dimensions of the work's organisation. A more detailed look at the exposition section of the Ballade indicates that there is a careful balance between developmental and closural tendencies both in the opening theme and in the section as a whole.

It is common for Chopin to open a work with a tonal anacrusis. Needless to say the Neapolitan quality of the A♭ major triad becomes clear only gradually, as other possibilities (I, ♭VI) are eliminated. The introduction here may be 'reduced' to an 8–1 descent which defines the G minor tonic only after Theme I is already under way. And it dovetails with Theme I in motivic as well as harmonic terms, as Ex. 13 indicates, giving a further analytical rationale to the e♭' in the chord of bar 7.[6] The quasi-cadential harmony appearing in mid-phrase gives a distinctive quality to Theme I, in sharp contrast to the richer dominant and diatonic sevenths which characterise the harmony of Theme II. It is worth looking a little more closely at the opening of Theme I. The remaining two notes of the theme – the falling major second (motive y) – are separated not only by Chopin's careful autograph phrasing, but by their placing after the cadential close to a G minor harmony. Significantly these two notes are a mirror of the opening two notes of the theme, so that motive x from the introduction is enclosed symmetrically by motive y and its mirror (Ex. 13). Already in these opening bars there is a nice balance of goal-directed progression and symmetry.

The second limb of Theme I at bar 36, signalled by the arrival of a postponed tonic, appears here for the only time in the work, though it is closely related to the later waltz episode. It establishes a continuity with the main part of the theme through its superimposition of x and y, but its main function is to generate tension and to effect a gradual transition from theme to figuration.

Example 14. First Ballade: (i) bars 8–9; (ii) bars 82–3

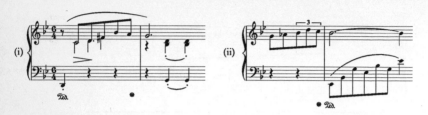

The figuration is then defined by the transition at 44 (still based on motive *y*), but its character changes at 56, as the arpeggiation takes on an accompanimental role, supporting the 'horn-call' motive which emerges at that point. The harmony here prepares the way for an expected resolution to the relative major and it is deflected to E♭ major only when the 'horn-call' is imperceptibly translated into the opening of Theme II.[7]

The entire paragraph is a triumphant essay in the art of transition, allowing subtle motivic connections and harmonic elisions to smooth the way from one idea to the next. Nor is this simply a matter of linking the two main themes. There is an imperceptible shading of function between theme, motive and figuration which is entirely typical of Chopin. And it should be noted that the shape outlined here is again a symmetry (Figure 6).

Bar	8	36	44	56	68
	theme	motive	figuration	motive	theme

Figure 6

The arch shape is reinforced, moreover, by the second limb of Theme II, a 'closing theme' which is in reality a transformation of Theme I, now in the major mode (Ex. 14).[8]

Musical structures may be 'read' in different ways and in several ways simultaneously. It is entirely possible for us to hear the waltz episode as the pinnacle of a thematic arch, while at the same time recognising a goal-directed momentum, achieved through waves of tension and release, which pulls strongly against this purely formal reading. At the heart of the First Ballade lies a fruitful counterpoint of shape and pattern, of process and form, and it operates at the level of the theme, of the paragraph and of the entire work. This formal ambivalence is an enriching aspect of the work, a measure indeed of its quality. Like most great music the Ballade is rich in ambiguities, implicative on several levels, wary of congruence, and dense with information.

Ballade No. 2, Op. 38

The essential dynamic of the Second Ballade is set up by the contrast between its two principal ideas, the first (Theme I) a siciliano melody in F major, which conceals its art beneath a deceptively innocent lilting surface (Ex. 3(i)) and the second (Theme II) a bravura figuration in A minor (Ex. 4(i)). Although contrast is the primary aim – and it is articulated by rhythm, texture and register as well as by tonal and thematic substance – Chopin establishes coherence by highlighting common ground between the two ideas. The F major of Theme I is inflected towards A minor (the tonal setting of Theme II) at bars 19–20, where it is part of a larger progression to V, and again at 37–8. Equally Theme II takes on the principal rhythmic cell of Theme I, notably between bars 63 and 67. More importantly there is a clear emphasis on *both* tonic pitch classes (A and F) within *each* tonal region, as the section bridging the final cadence of Theme I and the opening of Theme II (bars 42–6) clearly illustrates. The neighbour-note relation (F–E) built into the opening of Theme II is seminal, and is composed out on several levels of the work's tonal structure.

For all their shared elements, the contact between the two ideas is explosive (Ex. 4(i)), and its consequence is a carefully worked two-stage mediation. The first stage allows the figuration of Theme II to subside gradually and imperceptibly on to the siciliano melody of Theme I (bars 71–83). It does so by way of a temporary tonicisation of E♭ major, approached through its upper neighbour note in a manner which replicates the pattern at the opening of Theme II. A minor is denied tonic status by this progression and a chromatic sequence leads back to F major and the return of Theme I at bar 83.

On the face of it the Second Ballade is more distant from a sonata-form archetype than its predecessor. Yet the sonata-form plot is invoked unmistakably by several features of the musical argument. At bar 83 Theme I returns in the manner of a repeated exposition, only to allow a deceptive cadence at 96 to inaugurate an impassioned modulatory development section which is really the second stage of the two-stage mediation mentioned earlier. Here the siciliano melody is transformed to a point at which it can lead naturally into Theme II (bar 141). The process has been admirably described in an analysis by Wai-Ling Cheong,[9] who outlines two rising-fourth root progressions from 97 and 120. At the pivotal point – and at the centre of this development section – the opening bars of the siciliano melody return in an harmonic sequence which neatly represents the underlying tonal contrast between A minor and F major (through B and G majors, V of V in each region) (Ex. 15). The

Example 15. Second Ballade bars 116–23

harmonic function here is designed in part to ensure that the tonal destination remains as yet uncertain.

As in the G minor Ballade the reprise at bar 144 is marked by the return not of Theme I but of Theme II and again in its original tonal setting. Admittedly the harmonic context for the figuration – a $^6_4$ harmony on A – is subtly different from its initial presentation, but this actually strengthens the A minor tonality when it is made explicit at bar 149, since it creates a 'double suspension'.[10] And from this point A minor is secure, confirmed by the reappearance of material from Theme I (bar 157 onwards) and by a new bravura closing section (bar 169), where the F major key signature is finally cancelled. The closing section culminates in the return of Theme II, though, as in No. 1, the drive to the cadence is dramatically interrupted. Here the interruption is a final whispered reference to Theme I, now accommodated within the closing tonic of A minor in a gesture of synthesis which retains some element of sonata dialectic.

This outline of the design of the Ballade might be represented schematically as in Figure 7, with tonal centres indicating no more than points of departure and arrival. It is clear from the outline that the tonal centre of the Second Ballade shifts from an opening stable F major to a closing stable A minor. It is in short a two-key scheme. And since this is not common in early nineteenth-century music it may be helpful to examine it more closely. My analysis so far has been of an informal character, outlining the sequence of events and tracing something of the inner compositional logic which connects

	Bars	Tonality
Theme I	1–46	F major
Theme II	47–82	A minor
Theme I'	83–140	F major
Theme II'	141–68	A minor
Closing section (refs. to II and I)	169–204	A minor

Figure 7

them. Like every analysis it proceeds from certain theoretical premises, but these have not been made explicit. In considering the work's two-key scheme, however, I will step briefly beyond this informal presentation and engage with more formal theories of tonal structure.

It is indeed the two-key scheme which has consistently attracted attention to the Second Ballade in critical literature. Schumann – to whom the work was dedicated – remembered a monotonal version of the piece, ending as it began in F major, and without what he described as 'the impassioned episodes', by which he meant of course the figuration of Theme II.[11] We know from other sources that Chopin was in the habit of performing just the opening section of the work, and this is undoubtedly what he did in Schumann's presence. Speculation (by Gerald Abraham and others) about different stages in its creative process, involving either excisions or additions, is without any real documentary foundation.[12]

In a good deal of the critical writing on Chopin an association has been made between the Second Ballade and other works by him which have an emergent or directional tonal scheme (where the tonal destination becomes clear only gradually), notably the Op. 16 Rondo, the Bolero, the Mazurka Op. 30 No. 2, the Third Scherzo, the A minor Prelude, the Second Scherzo and the Fantasy Op. 49.[13] Several of these pieces are best described in analytical terms as monotonal (in a single key) with a non-tonic opening, and in style-historical terms as refinements of the tonally inductive prelude or recitative. It is possible indeed to identify several stages in Chopin's absorption of this recitative principle into his music, ranging from deceptive openings cleanly separated from the rest of the work, as in the E♭ major Rondo or the Bolero, to more integrated tonal pairings, as in the Second Scherzo and the Fantasy Op. 49.

It will be worth considering these latter works in more detail. In the Scherzo the initial B♭ minor establishes a structural tension with the main tonality of D♭ major, and this tension is later built into the tonal argument of the work. It is scarcely enough then to describe the opening (as Schenker does) as a tonal anacrusis.[14] Yet while the B♭–D♭ relation is seminal to the work, there is not much doubt about which region has priority. Contrary to the popular nomenclature, which names B♭ minor, this is indeed a Scherzo in D♭ Major. With the Fantasy Op. 49 the position is more complex. The weighting of the opening tonal region is such that a monotonal interpretation is more difficult to sustain. Yet even here, as Carl Schachter has demonstrated, there is a coherent large-scale progression towards the A♭ major goal, enabling the opening tonality, for all its structural importance, to take on a remote preparatory (i. e. unstable) or inductive quality.[15] It might be noted too that in both works the opening and closing regions are (conventionally) tonal relatives.

The Second Ballade takes the process a stage further. Here the alternation of clearly-defined F major and A minor regions (less closely related than the keys of Op. 49) refuses to permit a monotonal analysis. It can *only* be explained as a two-key scheme. This represents a significant departure from norms of structure in the early nineteenth century, and as such it raises analytical questions which are not so pertinent to the other works cited. It should perhaps be added that the two-key scheme need not entail a major departure from norms of perception, as many a listener will confirm,[16] nor indeed from norms of style, which are properly a subject of historical investigation.[17] Analysis does of course have a bearing on these issues, but its major competence as a discipline lies elsewhere. It is concerned less with effect or origin than with function, and its primary aim is to identify elements of structure in the terms of an underlying theory. In significant analytical work on the Second Ballade several such theories have been adopted.

One approach views the work against a background of monotonal theory. The most persuasive essays here have been those which adopt Schenkerian methods to explain the tonal scheme as a deviation from, or alternative to, monotonality. The classic texts are by Harald Krebs – his dissertation and subsequent article 'Alternatives to Monotonality in Early Nineteenth-century Music'.[18] Krebs interprets the Ballade as an interlocking of two controlling triads – F major and A minor – each with a 5–1 Fundamental Line. Kevin Korsyn, on the other hand, finds a 5–1 Fundamental Line for the F major material and a 3–1 for the A minor, so that C" forms a common Primary Tone.[19] There are other significant differences in the Schenkerian readings of Krebs and Korsyn, but their analytical researches are underpinned by a common theoretical premise, one which explains the tonal scheme deviationally in relation to the monotonality of classical practice.

It is less easy to make sense of Charles Rosen's claim that '[the] Second Ballade of Chopin (in F major/A minor), create[s] a tonal unity although a central tonality is not focused'.[20] This is part of Rosen's more general thesis that for the Romantics it was possible 'to integrate music in a general tonal area, rather than in a clearly defined and specific tonality'. He sees the 'mixture' of tonal relatives as especially significant here, remarking that 'for Chopin, in the F minor/A♭ major Fantasie and the B♭ minor/D♭ major Scherzo, they are more or less the same key'. Admittedly a tandem of tonal relatives is an important feature of style in Chopin, but this is a long way from describing them as 'more or less the same key'. Given the strong tonal contrasts which Chopin employs in these works, it is difficult to give this view much credence – still less any claim that the F major and A minor of the Second Ballade may form a 'tonal unity'.

A quite different analytical approach would be to propose a theory which can accommodate the two-key scheme in its own terms. One instance would be the 'interlocking tonal structures' proposed by Graham George.[21] Unfortunately George's own analyses founder on a simplistic notion of tonal closure and a failure even to consider how tonal processes unfold from one point to the next. Tonalities in short are viewed as closed, static (as opposed to time-dependent) entities. Nevertheless the double sequence of F major and A minor in the Second Ballade seems on the face of it to exemplify an 'interlocking tonal structure', albeit one in search of a more comprehensive theoretical formulation.

Such a formulation is offered in the work of Robert Bailey on Wagner and on post-Wagnerian symphonic structures.[22] Bailey is one of several theorists who identify in effect a second tonal system in the later nineteenth century, founded on a pairing of two tonics, coexisting rather than contrasting. They view this second tonal system as qualitatively different from classical tonality, having emerged in response to the diminished structural value of the dominant. Bailey's double-tonic complex – usually third-related – determines long-range tonal progressions not just in a surface way, but at a background level of tonal organisation comparable to that identified by Schenker. In these terms the Second Ballade might be viewed not as deviational from, but as an early exemplification of, the underlying theory, where the two keys form a third-related double-tonic complex and the directional element is one of shifting emphasis as between two co-existing elements. An essay on the Ballade along these lines is William Kinderman's 'Directional Tonality in Chopin'.[23]

One further approach may be considered – an examination of unifying elements in the pitch structure of the Ballade which remain independent of tonal harmonic functions. We might think here of the work done on fixed pitches in Liszt and Bartók by, among others, Stephen Emmerson, who demonstrates that the weakened structural role of traditional harmonic functions is to some extent compensated by a growing reliance on fixed pitches which have referential rather than controlling significance.[24] In his forthcoming book, *Tonal Deviation in Early Nineteenth-Century Music*, Harald Krebs addresses the Second Ballade from this viewpoint, arguing that the recurrence of four two-note groups (F–A, A–C, C–E and E–F) in both the opening and closing tonal areas contributes to coherence.[25]

These analytical approaches, through their systematic character, afford glimpses into the possible musical structures of the Second Ballade, their insights dependent upon, if not validated by, specific theoretical frameworks. There is nothing absolute about the findings here. Indeed precisely because of their often competing nature they return us to the more general point made at the outset of this chapter concerning the permeability of musical structure. This point was already implicit in my analysis of the First Ballade. By bringing theory to the fore in relation to the two-key scheme of the Second Ballade I make it explicit, and at the same time I underline the value of theory for analysis. It is theory above all which establishes the relativity of analytical work, mediating between the (potentially authoritarian) individual analysis and the (potentially permissive) multiplicity of possible analyses. Structure may indeed be permeable, but it is not infinitely so.

Ballade No. 3, Op. 47

The Third Ballade brings into focus the issue of compositional norms. Here Chopin deviates in fascinating ways from the conventions of sonata form, while at the same time establishing his dependence on those conventions. The alternative proposal that this Ballade is really a kind of rondo, by attributing a single function to the two (admittedly related) themes, seems eccentric to say the least.[26] In essence Chopin remodels the elements of sonata form by placing them in new contexts and subtly blending their traditionally separate formal functions. We may begin by establishing that there is a conventional opposition of primary and secondary themes and of primary and secondary tonal regions and that these are presented in a formal context which preserves the functions of exposition and reprise. Yet the inner dynamic which motivates the succession of events is far from conventional.

The exposition section may be presented schematically as in Figure 8.

	Bars	Tonality
Theme I	1–52	A♭ major
Theme II	53–115	F minor

Figure 8

Example 16. Third Ballade: (i) bars 50–4; (ii) bars 114–6; (iii) bars 155–7

Several commentators have been at pains to demonstrate the motivic links between these two themes, to the point of suggesting that the second is a variation or even inversion of the first.[27] Indeed the search for thematic unity has extended beyond the exposition section to embrace the work as a whole. There are undoubtedly unifying elements in the thematic substance of the Ballade, notably the falling second at the end of the first phrase, clearly separated (as in the First Ballade) by Chopin's own phrasing. And the scalar basis of the two main themes is a further obvious link. But it is rather easy to take this line of enquiry too far. The general claim of such motivic analysis is that structural coherence is achieved through a motivic interrelation of contrasting thematic elements or – more ambitiously – through the relationship of these elements to an underlying *Grundgestalt* (unifying basic shape). This is a large, not to say a rather strange, claim, and in practice many of the interconnections proposed for the Third Ballade, however ingenious, fail to

Example 17

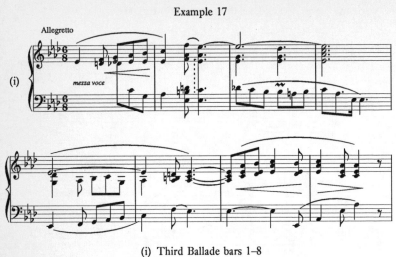

(i) Third Ballade bars 1–8

(ii) Third Ballade bars 47–9

support it, foundering on a reductive process whose terms of reference are by no means obvious. It is in any case of primary importance to explore the relationship between the two main themes on an exoteric level before broaching esoteric demonstrations of 'unity', a much abused term in criticism.

And on this less sophisticated level the themes do indeed have much in common. Above all they are both tonally and thematically 'enclosed'. Nor is there any conventional modulating section leading from one to the other. Theme I ends as it began in A♭ major and is linked to the F major harmony which opens Theme II by a single Schubertian pivot note (Ex. 16(i)). Theme II ends as it began with an F major harmony and the same pivot note translates this back to A♭ major for the beginning of the central episode (Ex. 16(ii)). It should be noted that since the central tonal region of Theme II is F *minor* (the real point of tonal arrival is bar 65, not 54), the tonal relationship between the two themes neatly inverts classical practice. The closed character of the themes is in turn heightened by their internal organisation. Each is contained within a tonal and thematic 'frame', and although the nature of the framing material is very different, it has the effect of separating out the two themes, encouraging us to view each of them in turn as a self-contained impulse of departure and return.

The shape of the themes may now be examined more closely. The opening eight-bar sentence of the Ballade conceals beneath its lyrical surface a subtle contrapuntal organisation, in which the melody travels from top voice to bass (bars 1–4) and from bass to top voice (5–8) (Ex. 17(i)). One feature alone remains implicative. Through the resources of invertible counterpoint the bass is assigned two of the three motivic strands which make up the melody. When the opening sentence returns as a closing frame at bar 37, this implication is realised, and Theme I closes with the remaining motive as a unison in the bass (Ex. 17(ii)). This considerably strengthens the sense of closure for the theme as a whole. The intervening material (9–36) is developmental in character, based on the falling second of Ex. 17(i) – the unifying element noted earlier – and it unfolds through a chain of motivic connections in an accelerating pattern of phrase lengths.[28]

Theme II takes over the iambic rhythm which dominated Theme I and exaggerates its distinctive lilt by harmonising the weak beat rather than the strong. In so doing it generates an insistent, reiterative quality which makes implicit demands on the later stages of the musical argument. Again the opening section (bars 52–65) returns at the end (103–15) to frame the main theme. Unlike the opening of Theme I, however, the introductory section of Theme II functions as a structural upbeat, arriving at the main tonal region of F minor only at bar 65 – and even then the F minor tends towards the overall tonic of A♭ major at 69 and 85. With the arrival of F minor Chopin presents the major strand of Theme II and immediately repeats it in a more impassioned guise at bar 81. This lends to the theme as a whole the following 'enclosed' structure (Figure 9).

Bar	52	65	81	103
	A	B	B'	A

Figure 9

The return of Theme II at bar 144 has been described as the beginning of a powerful development section.[29] It is true that the theme unfolds in a new tonal area and that it is built to a point of considerable intensity. But it has also been argued that it is the first stage of a mirror reprise, following the practice of the First and Second Ballades.[30] The theme is indeed presented unaltered and in its entirety (apart from the final 'frame'). And the avoidance of the conventional key was already a feature of the first two ballades at the reprise of Theme II, as was the 'aggrandisement' of the theme on repetition. This ambivalence is a calculated property of the formal design, which invokes the classical model only to subvert it in several ways. The pivot note which introduces this statement of Theme II is now A♭, maintaining an obvious continuity with earlier stages of the tonal argument, and the introductory section (A in the diagram above) treats this – as before – as a dominant. It resolves enharmonically at 157 to C♯ minor, the first moment in the work where we leave the orbit of A♭ major/F minor (Ex. 16(iii)).

There is considerable intensification of the material at this stage, achieved not through ornamentation but through a succession of new textural backgrounds. Initially (bar 156) the second part of Theme II (B in Figure 9) is given a left-hand semiquaver 'accompaniment', though this term is wholly inadequate to describe the beautifully moulded counter-theme which winds its chromatic way through two expressive arcs of melody. For the completion of B the main theme then moves into the left hand (compare the initial presentation of Theme I) while a top-voice dominant pedal (G♯) again connects enharmonically with the A♭ major of the earlier stages of the work. The climax comes with the repetition of the main theme (B') in a 'fully scored' version at bar 173. As so often in Chopin (compare the C minor Nocturne Op. 48 No. 1) the reprise here assumes something of the character of an apotheosis.

There is a comparable reprise of Theme I at bar 213, again in the full-textured manner of an apotheosis, and as in the First Ballade this also coincides with the tonal reprise. The reprise of the two themes can now be represented as in Figure 10.

	Bars	*Tonality*
Theme II'	144–183	C♯ minor
Theme I'	213–230	A♭ major

Figure 10

It is when we consider the 'gaps' in Figures 8 and 10 that we become fully aware of the extent to which Chopin has reinterpreted the normative functions of sonata form. The first of these gaps is the section separating the end of the exposition and the beginning of the reprise of Theme II (bars 116–144). The expectation here would of course be a development section, thematically and tonally unstable. But Chopin gives us instead an independent episode (Theme

Example 18. Third Ballade bars 124–5

III) which remains firmly in the tonic key of A♭ major and thus has none of the quality of a development. Indeed it is mainly for this reason that the reprise of Theme II can rather easily be interpreted as the beginning of a development section.

The episode falls into three sections and its major function is to provide a contrast to the unremitting iambic rhythm of Themes I and II. The major contrast is provided by the second of the three sections (bars 124–35), a non-recurring 'quick waltz' theme characterised by moto perpetuo arabesques and supported by trochaic rather than iambic rhythms (Ex. 18). It might be compared with the 'waltz' in the First Ballade (Ex. 1(i)), and it has a similar pivotal placing. Once more a waltz episode forms the central pinnacle of a formal arch, flanked by the exposition and the mirror reprise. The first and third sections of the episode mediate between the waltz theme and its surroundings. Thus the first section (116–23) introduces the semiquaver movement of the waltz, but preserves an iambic accompaniment based on the all-important falling second of Theme I. It is this music which in due course brings the Ballade to a triumphant close, returning unexpectedly after the reprise of Theme I (bar 231). The third section (136–44) in turn links the waltz to the reprise of Theme II by preparing that theme melodically.

It remains to consider the 'gap' between the reprise of Theme II and the reprise of Theme I (bars 183–212). And here, for the first time in the work, we encounter the thematic working and modulatory sequences associated with an archetypal development section, though the placing of this is of course unorthodox. The effect is to heighten the ambivalence between a formal symmetry (centred on Theme III) and a goal-directed sonata movement, an ambivalence which had already played a major part in the First Ballade. Chopin's thematic treatments during this development section are indeed remarkable. In essence he fuses the opening phrases of Theme II and Theme I into a single melodic shape which is then treated sequentially, before a subtle transformation enables the return to A♭ major and the reprise of Theme I (bar

213). An overall outline of the formal design of the Ballade may now be presented (Figure 11).

	Bars	Tonality
Theme I	1–52	A♭ major
Theme II	53–115	F minor
Theme III	116–144	A♭ major
Theme II'	144–183	C♯ minor
Theme II+I	183–212	modulatory
Theme I' (refs. to Theme III)	213–241	A♭ major

Figure 11

Even those commentators who insist on the need to avoid any reference to sonata form in relation to the ballades make constant use of its terminology in their interpretation of this sequence. In doing so they implicitly recognise the importance of sonata form as a controlling principle, albeit one which has been reinterpreted to the point at which there may be significant disagreement about the labelling of formal functions. Some have argued that the end of the exposition should be placed at bar 144 rather than 115; others that the beginning of the development should be at 144 rather than 183. Naturally events may be susceptible to more than one interpretation. But the importance of compositional norms lies in their capacity to establish interpretative codes which will make some readings of the form more profitable than others.

It is all too easy to argue that in the Third Ballade the departures from a sonata-form schema are so radical that it is no longer helpful to invoke the schema. More realistic is the view that the Ballade unfolds against a background of existing norms, from which it derives much of its essential meaning, but that the deviations from those norms in turn contribute to the tentative establishment of new norms. This latter development, which really broaches the question of generic definition, will be a major concern of my final chapter. But it may be remarked even at this stage that the formal interpretation of the Third Ballade offered in these pages depends not only (though principally) on a recognition of the conventions of a classical sonata, but also on some assessment of the conventions of a new genre, the Chopin ballade.

Ballade No. 4, Op. 52

In the first and third ballades Chopin enriched his sonata-based structures by counterpointing them against the formal symmetry of an arch design. In the Fourth Ballade there is a similar purposeful ambivalence. But here the

Example 19. Fourth Ballade reduction bars 1–7

directional qualities of a sonata are counterpointed against the 'static' repetition structure of a variation set. Sonata form is suggested by the thematic and tonal dualism of the exposition, where Theme I is presented in the tonic (F minor) and Theme II in the subdominant major, B♭. But the mirror reprise of the other three ballades is replaced here by a more orthodox sequence in which Theme I returns in the tonic and Theme II is modified tonally to appear in the submediant major. Variation form is in turn suggested by the successive treatments of Theme I. This blending of different formal functions influences both the large-scale design and the more detailed organisation of the work. On the larger scale it accounts in part for the absence of a conventional development section, so that the overall design is bipartite. On the smaller scale it has major implications for the character of the thematic exposition.

Characteristically Chopin approaches the main theme obliquely. The introduction (bars 1–7) outlines a dominant harmony (suggesting the major rather than the minor mode) which prepares Theme I through the composing-out of a simple triadic descent (Ex. 19). At the same time it establishes an important relationship with Theme I based on its opening four repeated notes, a relationship which is later exploited to facilitate the unexpected return of the introduction at 129. Finally it prepares us at the outset for the foreground contrapuntal procedures which are a special characteristic of this ballade.[31] The contrapuntal intricacies are highlighted in Chopin's autograph 'scoring' of the introduction, as indicated in Ex. 10.

Theme I (bars 7–71) is an extended multi-sectional paragraph, whose organisation already owes something to variation-form. The basic material is presented as a tripartite structure (7–22), whose short-breathed phrases and internal repetitions cohere into an indivisible whole due to the unobtrusive asymmetries of the phrase structure and the compelling sweep of the underlying harmonic movement. In the three statements of the opening phrase the first parts of the phrase (antecedents) are always harmonically enclosed and the second parts (consequents) always progressive. On its first presentation the consequent progresses to the relative major (bar 12), enabling Chopin to restate the phrase in that region. This time the consequent

Example 20. Fourth Ballade reduction bars 8–22

progresses from A♭ major to a subdominant harmony of B♭ minor. In this region the phrase can return at its original pitch (bar 18) but supported by an F *major* (rather than minor) harmony – in other words functioning as a local dominant rather than a tonic. And the effect of this reprise at bar 18 is the more striking for its dislocation of phrase structure. The consequent on this occasion returns us to the home dominant. The entire process, in which a thematic reprise at the original pitch is taken in as part of a broader harmonic progression, is summarised in Ex. 20. It may be noted that the theme points both to the conventional secondary tonality of A♭ (eventually established in the middle section) and the actual secondary tonality of B♭ (established by Theme II).

Unusually Chopin then repeats this entire sequence in a slightly varied form (Variation I) (bars 23–36). The melodic variants here are of little significance in themselves, offering the merest hint of the decorative treatments which will come in the reprise. Rather it is the element of tonal and thematic repetition which suggests that variation form will play an important part in the structure of the Ballade. This statement is in turn followed by a further episode, again a variation of Theme I but developmental rather than decorative in character, and harmonically significant because of its upper neighbour-note inflection to V of B♭. This section (37–57) effectively strengthens the general tendency of the Ballade to gravitate towards the subdominant. The overall progression from this G♭ major harmony to the return of the tonic at bar 58 is outlined in Ex. 21. Although based on the main theme, this section offers a necessary element of contrast to the repetition structures surrounding it. It also introduces a pronounced contrapuntal element in the working of one of the main motives of Theme I.

The contrapuntal dimension is taken further in the variation of Theme I which immediately follows (bars 58–71). This (Variation II) returns to the tonal and thematic repetitions of the earlier presentations, but for the first time in the work it builds in intensity towards a major climax at bar 72, mainly

Example 21. Fourth Ballade reduction bars 34–58

IV   V——I

through the offices of a countermelody in constant semiquaver movement. As before, the variation reaches a subdominant region (B♭ minor), established through its dominant. The non-thematic arc of figuration (72–80) character-istically defers a tonic resolution, however, acting as a 'transition' which can absorb the head of tension built up by the variation in preparation for the B♭ major of Theme II (bar 80). At this point the several tendencies to the subdominant region are fully realised. Generically Theme II partakes of a double character – barcarolle and chorale. And in these terms the sequence of 'slow waltz' and 'barcarolle' echoes that of Op. 23.

The overall organisation of the exposition may be presented as in Figure 12.

	Bars	Tonality
Introduction	1–7	
Theme I	7–22	F minor
Variation I	23–36	
Episode based on Theme I	37–57	
Variation II	58–71	
Transition	72–80	
Theme II	80–99	B♭ major

Figure 12

At this point a development section would be expected in the conventional sonata movement. There is indeed a short middle section (bars 99–134) and it contains the modulatory sequences characteristic of a development. Yet functionally it lacks the weight – the structural tension and instability – of an archetypal development section, and also its dependence on the material presented in the exposition. Indeed in character this section offers some of the few relatively lightweight moments in the work. It is easier to understand the section as an extended bridge between the exposition and reprise, affording necessary contrast but not demanding resolution or synthesis. It is made up

Example 22. Fourth Ballade bars 121–3

of three structures, of which the first two rely largely on sequential treatment
of figurative patterns, while at the same time directing the music increasingly
towards the conventional secondary region of A♭ major. This is established by
the third structure at bar 121. Retrospectively it may also be related (as V)
to the D♭ major reprise of Theme II.

The journey from this point to the reprise is one of the most magical passages
in Chopin. The main strands of Theme I are here isolated and presented in
contrapuntal combination, as Ex. 22 indicates. Moreover one of these strands
is gradually and beautifully transformed into the unobtrusive return of the
introduction in the remote foreground region of A major, a transition made
possible by the shared repeated notes of the introduction and Theme I. This
is the mid-point of the structure. By treating the A major as a dominant and
elaborating it in a cadenza, Chopin then enables his reprise to begin in the
unexpected key of D minor (bar 135).

This represents a further variation of Theme I (Variation III), and one which
fulfils all the canonic aspirations of earlier material (indeed much of the
dynamic of the work can be understood in terms of the progressive
'polyphonicisation' of its principal thematic material). The tonal setting of the
reprise proves ingeniously deceptive, exploiting the minor third sequence
built into Theme I to return the music very quickly to the tonic. The canonic
element is thus absorbed unobtrusively into the harmonic flow of the original
material. A final variation of Theme I (Variation IV) follows at bar 152, this
time extending an implication of Variation I to develop a cantabile-decorative
treatment of exquisitely moulded ornamental melody. It is the moment at
which the entire work seems to flower, with the nocturne-like fioriture
reaching ever higher and in ever more daring transformations of the original.

The overall tonal direction suggested by the music at this point is again
towards the subdominant and the ornamental variation builds steadily towards
a dominant preparation of B♭ major. In the end Theme II is repeated not in

that key but in D♭ major. This is a dramatic moment in the larger tonal structure and it may be as well to elaborate on it at this stage. It has been noted that there is a tendency to the subdominant in the presentation of Theme I and that this is eventually affirmed by the tonal setting of Theme II in the exposition. Against this background the D♭ major of the reprise takes on special power and significance. Carl Schachter has argued persuasively not just that the D♭ harmony replaces an expected B♭, but that it remains within the orbit and control of a subdominant region which was established at bar 160 and reaches through to 195.[32] Schachter goes on to comment on the 'profound irony' which enables this precarious harmonic support to underpin a passage of such major climactic importance.

It is indeed a glorious moment. The deceptive innocence of Theme II is transformed into a powerful apotheosis, building with ever more impassioned fervour towards the moment at which a ⁶₄ harmony on C once again signals the return to F minor. The structural dominant appears now for the first time in the work and it remains suspended, poised on a precipice of harmonic tension, while a series of pianissimo chords prolongs it in a brief illusion of repose. The bravura closing section which follows seems to exorcise earlier conflicts and tensions in a white heat of virtuosity. These final moments are among the most majestic perorations in all Chopin.

The overall structure of the ballade may now be outlined as in Figure 13.

	Bars	Tonality
Introduction	1–7	
Theme I	7–22	F minor
Variation I	23–36	
Episode based on Theme I	37–57	
Variation II	58–71	
Transition	72–80	
Theme II	80–99	B♭ major
Episode/Development (Theme I)	99–128	A♭ major
Introduction	129–34	
Theme I		
Variation III	135–51	F minor
Variation IV	152–68	
Theme II	169–210	D♭ major
Closing section (Theme III)	211–39	F minor

Figure 13

It may be as well to offer some general comment on the presentation of Figure 13, since formal synopses of this kind have played some part in my analysis throughout this chapter. Undoubtedly these outlines are helpful in summarising analytical observations and offering rough-and-ready guides to the sequence of events in a work. Their practical advantages for a study such as this probably outweigh their conceptual limitations. All the same we should be aware of those limitations. The main difficulty is that these outlines present musical structures in an entirely one-dimensional way, where all components are treated rather like static entities on a single level of formal significance. They ignore the time-dependency of musical structures, their 'unfolding' through progressive and recessive textures on several levels. And they are quite unable to account for the hierarchies, the embedded or 'nested' structures, which lie at the heart of tonal music.

I have tried to convey something of this multi-levelled richness and complexity by the verbal commentaries of this chapter. But verbal commentaries have their limitations too. Hence the need felt by so many analysts to develop tools which can cope with those very qualities which resist explication through simple tabulation or verbal description. Already in my discussion of individual ballades there has been some recourse to formal theories of tonal music which set out to penetrate the structural core of the music. The final chapter, which examines the four ballades collectively, will continue to draw freely on such theories, and it will also seek help occasionally from the theory and analysis developed within cognate disciplines.

4

Genre

Theories

'In Scherzi, Ballades, Polonoises (sic), Preludes etc. the individual character of each rarely fails to be admirably maintained.' This was the view of the critic of *The Athenaeum* in his obituary of Chopin (27 October 1849). His remark returns us to the concept of genre, which must now be addressed more fully.

Before considering the Chopin ballade as a genre it may be helpful to prepare the ground by looking briefly at theoretical perspectives on genre. Theories of genre – addressing definition, function and causes – have a lengthy, even an ancient, pedigree in literary studies and they have found a place in musicology too.[1] In the widest understanding of the term a genre is defined not only by formal and stylistic properties, but also by social context.[2] And in this sense we might regard the lyric piano piece of the early nineteenth century as an undivided genre, its evolution and characteristic profile heavily dependent on a particular validating community, and its multiple titles carrying a collective connotation. Within the terms of this broad definition Chopin might well be regarded as one of the most persuasive advocates of an emergent genre, and his titles are entirely characteristic. However, we learn little from this perspective about the status of the ballade.

A narrower understanding of genre would locate both primary causes and classifications in the inherent materials of an art, without reference to social context. In their studies of literature, for example, the influential literary critics and theorists of Russian Formalism (working mainly in the 1920s on the formal properties of literary texts) understood generic evolution as part of a more general process of stylistic evolution, governed above all by the principle of 'struggle and succession'.[3] This is presented as a dialectical process, internal to the art, in which the dominant or canonised line comes into conflict with coexisting minor lines and is eventually overthrown by these minor lines, now duly canonised. New genres emerge, then, as accumulating minor devices acquire a focus and challenge the major line. Despite its literary origins this aspect of Russian Formalist theory maps rather well against Chopin's stylistic evolution and in particular his transformation of elements drawn from post-classical popular concert music.[4] The qualitative change – the point at which the devices of a 'minor line' acquired a focus – occurred in the Vienna and early Paris years, and it inaugurated a *major* line within nineteenth-century piano music.

Chopin's genre titles – including 'ballade' – worked to formalise this change of style at a transitional moment in music history. Since it is the role of genre – within Formalist theory – notionally to categorise musical experience, to close or finalise it, the 'new' will tend to remain weakly defined until accumulating changes in style and form are ready to be validated by genre. Hence the generic permissiveness of much early nineteenth-century piano music, evident in the remarkable profusion of genre titles, often used casually and even interchangeably, and at times emanating from the publisher rather than the composer. In Formalist terms Chopin's project was to create a generic order amidst the free-ranging devices of this emergent repertory. Unlike many of his early-romantic contemporaries, he did not select his titles arbitrarily or use them loosely in his mature music. They had specific, though not necessarily conventional, generic meanings, established through an internal consistency in the semiotic relation of the title to the formal and stylistic features of the piece.

The title is integral to the piece and partly conditions our response to its formal and stylistic content, but it does not create a genre. Equally a classification of formal and stylistic devices will not of itself establish a consistent basis for generic differentiation (consider the substantial overlaps between Chopin's genres). It is the interaction of title and content which creates generic meaning. And here a social dimension re-enters the debate, enhancing our understanding of the function of genre within validating communities. As several authors have noted in literary and musical theory, a genre behaves rather like a contract between author and reader, composer and listener, a contract which may be broken.[5] The content in short may subvert the signal sent by the title. This subversion, which naturally depends on some measure of correspondence between title and content, can actually strengthen a generic definition, clarifying its terms through their temporary falsification. As the major cultural theorist and sociologist Theodor Adorno (with Max Horkheimer, a leading member of the so-called 'Frankfurt School') expressed it: 'Universals such as genres ... are true to the extent that they are subject to a countervailing dynamic.'[6]

Adorno's understanding of genre offers indeed an intriguing complement to

the Formalist view. For Adorno the dialectic of generic evolution is not between major and minor lines but between Universal and Particular, where deviations from a schema in turn generate new schemata. And even when genres have achieved conventional status, validated by consensus, their full meaning continues to depend on a dialectic of norms and deviations. Generic codes in this sense form part of a larger 'complex of meaning', and this may operate even within the work of a single composer, provided that there is enough stability in signification to enable a schema to accommodate notable deviation.

These approaches by the Russian Formalists and by Adorno have an obvious bearing on the stability – even the legitimacy – of the Chopin ballade as a genre. Viewed diachronically, it might be argued that the ballade evolved in counterpoint to sonata-form norms, with each successive ballade strengthening an emerging generic definition. Viewed synchronically, the four ballades might be regarded as a closed system defined through a network of norms and deviations. From either perspective the claim would be that the Chopin ballade is a controlling genre, which the individual piece exemplifies as well as making its own statement.

Chopin did indeed value genre as a force for conformity, stability and closure, a channel through which the work might seek a fixed and final meaning. At the same time the work in its uniqueness resists any such finalisation of meaning and the unity which that implies. And this leads to yet another aspect of genre study in Chopin, narrower still in its focus on segments rather than wholes. Through a concern with interpretative codes as well as compositional strategies, this approach departs from the Formalists and Adorno alike to invoke a cluster of ideas loosely gathered by the term 'Post-Structuralism'. Here the issue of norms and deviations takes on new significance. As well as temporary negations of a prevailing norm, deviations from *that* norm may well be partial affirmations of alternative norms, particles which signify absent wholes. And this has special relevance to one of the most notable aspects of Chopin's art, its persistent allusion to genres outside the main controlling genre of a work.

It calls for comment that these generic referents are usually distanced from the instrumental traditions of high art music. They are either vocal genres, especially from opera, or, and more commonly, popular genres – march, funeral march, waltz, mazurka, barcarolle, chorale. We have already noted an ancestry for this eclecticism in post-classical concert music. Yet the counterpoint of genres in Chopin reaches far beyond anything in that repertory, prising open the closed meanings of host or controlling genres to

forge links with other moments in his own music and beyond. Indeed much of the expressive quality of Chopin's music is directly attributable to this play on popular genres, and it often lies at the root of the descriptive and even programmatic interpretations favoured by nineteenth- and early twentieth-century critics.

By assuming a parenthetical role in a Chopin work, popular genres – with their residue of social function – are given boundaries and placed in a dialogue with an autonomous art music. Yet Chopin's was still an art of synthesis and integration. Having admitted elements from different genres into a single work, he carefully blurred their edges, allowing them to blend and interpenetrate. And having proposed a separation of popular genres and art music, he proceeded to mediate constantly between them.

All this has a direct bearing on the ballades, where 'waltz' and 'barcarolle' elements convey something of the characteristic ambivalence I have described, at once separated out and integrated. But these elements carry an additional significance in the ballades, and one which draws together Formalist and Post-Structuralist perspectives. On the one hand they are constituents of a referential code which cuts across generic boundaries. On the other hand they function as 'markers' or 'dominants' of the controlling genre, since they are among the principal features which forge cyclic links between the four works. These links in their turn work to establish a generic definition.

Cycles

Three of Chopin's genres comprise four pieces each – the Scherzo, Impromptu and Ballade. Even the chronologies are similar, with the first essay in each genre dating from the mid-1830s and the last from 1842. In each case he established a private definition of the genre through an internal consistency in the correspondence between title and content. This involved giving a new definition to a conventional title (the Scherzo), defining for the first time a title which carried little generic meaning when he first used it (the Impromptu),[7] and establishing a new title for piano music (the Ballade). For all three genres we can establish normative elements – embracing dimensions, formal design, phraseology, and a repertory of specific gestures – which interlock across the four pieces. And for all three we can identify purposeful deviations which strengthen the norms and carry much of the expressive burden of the music.[8]

Cyclic links of a motivic kind have been proposed for the ballades. The falling second motive, carefully isolated by Chopin in both the First and Third

Example 23. Generic themes

First Ballade

Second Ballade

Third Ballade

Fourth Ballade

ballades, is a specific link, and it can be argued that the same motive operates at a deeper structural level in No. 2 as well. Neil Witten has also drawn attention to characteristic melodic shapes such as the 2–3–1 melodic endings and the movement from 6 to 5 which is prominent in many of the themes.[9] There are further gestures, such as the 'upbeats' to Theme I of No. 2 and Theme II of No. 3, which seem to invite cross-reference. Yet it is in the basic character, rather than the motivic substance, of their thematic materials that the ballades are most obviously part of a single genre. All four works have a similar metrical structure – 6/4 in No. 1 (apart from the closing section) and 6/8 in the others (originally 6/4 in No. 4). The flowing 'narrative' manner of this compound duple rhythm has often attracted comment, and it will be discussed in due course. But it might be noted at this stage that the metrical structure is not unrelated to the generic character of the themes. Already in No. 1 there is a relatively clear differentiation of thematic 'characters', or 'topics', to use Leonard Ratner's term.[10] The two main themes establish discreet 'slow waltz' and 'barcarolle' referents, while the third theme is an explicit 'quick waltz'. In addition there is recitative material, figuration (transitional or buffer-like in function) and a bravura closing section.

There is a kind of sequence flowing from this through the other three works. The barcarolle referent of No. 1 is accentuated in the main theme of No. 2, where it becomes in effect a siciliano. And figuration here is elevated to thematic status. The barcarolle material is taken up again in the two main themes of No. 3, and so too is the quick waltz of No. 1, together with its pivotal function in the structure. The slow waltz and barcarolle referents of No. 1 are strikingly duplicated in No. 4, which also employs recitative and figurative material. Ex.23 illustrates a derivation chain based on the barcarolle/siciliano material, while Figure 14 presents some of the generic links diagrammatically.

	recit	slow waltz	figuration	barcarolle/siciliano	quick waltz
Op. 23	intro	Theme I	middle/closing sections	Theme II	Theme III
Op. 38			Theme II/closing section	Theme I	
Op. 47			middle section	Theme I/II	Theme III
Op. 52	intro/cadenza	Theme I	middle/closing sections	Theme II	

Figure 14

Formally too there are strong arguments for a generic association between the four works. The Chopin ballade might be located somewhere between a sonata and a fantasy. Glib though it undoubtedly is, this description captures the ballade's dependence on, and at the same time its 'stretching' of, the sonata-form archetype. The uniqueness of the ballade as a genre is measured against the sonata-form norms which its formal successions continue to invoke. Special interpretations of sonata form are a useful framework, then, for a continuing exploration of cyclic elements.

The First Ballade establishes a formal model, of which selected aspects are then elaborated by the later ballades. To an extent then our understanding of the individual work can be enhanced by our knowledge of a collective practice. Despite the difference in tone, the Second Ballade establishes a clear formal and procedural relationship with the First. Again there are two generic themes – siciliano and étude – which are closer in style to a post-classical concert repertory than to the normative classical or early-romantic sonata. Again the tonal relationship between the two themes is unconventional, with the major-mode theme once more a major third below the minor-mode theme. Again the development functions in part as a thematic synthesis, building Theme I to the point at which it collides with Theme II (cf. bar 106 in No. 1 and 141 in No. 2). Again the reprise begins with Theme II in its original key, inaugurating a mirror reprise which is not in the end completed either tonally or thematically. And again there is a bravura closing section with a contrasting rhythmic character.

In the Third Ballade the generic character of the two themes relates more obviously to No. 2 than to No. 1, though in motivic substance Theme I is closer to No. 1. Once more the tonal relationship between the themes is unorthodox and third-related, here a reversal of the normal classical practice for a *minor*-mode sonata-allegro movement. The parallel with the First Ballade extends, moreover, to the 'quick waltz' central episode based on figuration (Theme III), lighter in tone than surrounding material, and the formal symmetry is emphasised again by a mirror reprise. As in No. 1 the reprise of Theme II is in the character of an apotheosis, and here a similar treatment is afforded to Theme I. The mirror reprise is interrupted by a development section which again draws the two themes together, this time actually welding them into a 'new' composite theme.

The Fourth Ballade returns to the tonally inductive introduction of the first. Here too the introduction has motivic links with Theme I and returns unexpectedly in the course of the work. The generic characters of the two themes are also similar to those of No. 1, a 'slow waltz' and 'barcarolle' respectively, and the tonal relation between them is once more unconventional. As in the First and Third Ballades the middle section has a (relatively) lightweight character involving figuration. This is the only ballade without a mirror reprise, but like Nos. 1 and 3 it has an apotheotic reprise (of both themes), and like No. 1 it has a bravura closing section.

All four ballades conspicuously rethink the tonal practice of the classical sonata. With the qualified exception of No. 4 they avoid the double reprise – tonal and thematic – which is characteristic of the classical sonata-allegro movement, and they are scrupulous in their avoidance of a conventional I–V (major mode) or I–III (minor mode) exposition. Indeed the rejection of V as a means of articulating formal units is profoundly significant, and it touches on the most significant of all the cyclic links between the ballades – a common approach to large-scale tonal organisation. The matter will be explored in a later section, but it should be remarked here that the absence of a conventional tonal dialectic in the exposition and the avoidance of a monotonal reprise in the tonic encourage us to regard the reprise as apotheosis rather than synthesis. If anything it is in the development sections that some element of synthesis occurs.

This has an important bearing on the larger general shape of these works. Apart from the Second Ballade, they tend to be end-weighted. The earlier stages are kept at a low temperature and tension is built gradually but inexorably towards the final moments when the tonic is reaffirmed in a moment of catharsis. In the first, third and fourth ballades the dynamic reworkings of a sonata-form model are directed above all towards the articulation of this fundamental 'plot archetype', to return to Anthony Newcomb's potent phrase. In contrast the Second Ballade is concerned with the integration of an initial explosive contrast. It is in this respect above all that the Second Ballade might be regarded as the (confirming) deviation from a generic norm. But there are other ways in which it stands a little way outside the territory marked out by the other three ballades, notably in its two-key scheme, its figurative second theme, and its formal 'intercutting' of contrasting materials rather than (or as well as) cumulative variation and transformation of related materials.

On one level, then, shared characteristics interlock across all four pieces in a manner which strongly suggests a derivation chain. On another level norms are established by three of the four pieces, while the fourth deviates from these norms within certain limits. In this way the ballades offer a small-scale model of the workings of a conventional genre. It is clear that they inhabit the same generic world; that the title meant something rather specific to Chopin. It would be easy to overstate the case, however. A ballade is not a conventional genre such as a sonata, where the specific expectations created by the title serve, paradoxically, to throw uniqueness into the sharpest possible relief.[11] Since the ballade has no conventional definition, the *absence* of specific expectations serves, again paradoxically, to throw cyclic elements into relief. Unlike the sonata, the title ballade makes few *a priori* demands on the musical material. If it had a single contemporary connotation it was with the notion of a 'story'. This may be a linking feature, but it is one which again promotes the particular (the content) rather than the universal (the plot).

It is tempting to draw an analogy with the rather later genre 'symphonic poem'. Here too the music often made its points against the background of conventional formal models, depending heavily for its expressive value on a force-field between the (abstract) model and the (concrete) work. With the symphonic poem deviations from the model would, however, be interpreted in the light of a particular programme, focusing much of the non-musical 'story' in musical terms. Such programmes are not of course part of the property of the Chopin ballades. Yet the genre title invites us to explore the force-field between norms and deviations in something like these terms. That force-field helps establish cyclic relations between the four ballades. As I will later demonstrate, it also encourages us to spin a 'narrative thread' for each ballade in turn.

Structures

In considering the ballades as a genre I have examined cyclic associations based on metre, thematic character and formal design. It is worth asking to what extent the four works demonstrate comparable associations at a deeper structural level. Since tonal structures are by definition hierarchical, and their hierarchies may be registered even at the remotest background level of a work, they offer for many of us the best hope of hearing the work as a unified totality, where the part is related organically to the whole. For this reason I will concentrate here on tonal structures, though I will first offer some brief observations on thematic process.

Reference has been made to a body of analytical writing which investigates the role of 'basic shape' in Chopin by tracing the unifying threads linking diverse themes. Much of this research has been summarised by Anatoly Leikin, who adds his own analytical insights to the corpus. Such work can be illuminating. Indeed Leikin's remarks on the thematic integration of the Third Ballade are themselves of analytical value, demonstrating not only the inversional relation of Themes I and II, but also the sense in which the opening of Theme I is 'completed' by Theme II and the nature of some of the inner-voice connections between these themes and the central episode.[12] Yet this form of analysis can be susceptible to indiscipline and even self-deception, especially where the criteria used to reduce a passage or a work to essential unifying shapes remain ill-defined. As David Epstein rightly observes, subsequent analysts distorted, by greatly simplifying, Schoenberg's notion of *Grundgestalt* (basic unifying shape),[13] and any analytical exercise along these lines might reasonably begin by attempting to recover that notion. More germane to present purposes, the value of such an exercise is in no sense specific to the ballades in Chopin's output, and will lend little support to any hypothesis about their status as a genre.

A more fruitful line of enquiry concerns the variation and transformation processes at work in the ballades, since, as Anna Bogdańska suggests,[14] there are features here that do seem closely associated with, though certainly not unique to, the ballades. The thematic process of these works is entirely in keeping with their goal-directed qualities, in which a steady growth of intensity culminates in a final apotheosis. It may be focused with reference to classical thematic development on the one hand and Lisztian thematic transformation on the other.

As in the classical sonata there is segmentation and recomposition of themes in the ballades. But it is directed to rather different ends. The motives of a normative classical development section are functionally incomplete in that they invite us to remember their original context as parts of closed themes and to anticipate their return to this context. As such they are major devices of temporal progression, taking us from one area of relative structural stability to another. In the Chopin ballades, on the other hand, the segmentation of themes has a more localised role. It may be an agent of intensification within a main thematic group (No. 1 bar 36); a function of transition (No. 4 bar 121); even a gesture of thematic synthesis (No. 2 bar 157; No. 3 bar 183). But in each case the thematic segmentation is part of, and absorbed within, a larger continuous process of evolution and variation.

As in some late nineteenth-century music, notably of the Liszt circle, there is thematic transformation in the ballades. But again there are important differences in application and function. Thematic transformation in Liszt involves the replacement of one closed theme with another (a disguised form of the first), so that it carries with it few implications for temporal progression. In the Chopin ballades transformation processes are cumulative, concerned with the gradual enrichment of a theme through variation, textural expansion and contrapuntal intensification. Material seldom returns in its original state, though the processes of variation may affect only minor details. They may involve matters of accompaniment rather than substance (No. 1 bars 22–5; No. 3 bar 157); minor melodic changes (No. 1 bars 114 and 170; No. 4 bar 24); ornamental elaboration (No. 4 bar 152); and, most important, progressive textural amplification (No. 1 bars 67, 105 and 166; No. 2 bars 12 and 111; No. 3 bars 1, 45 and 213; No. 4 bars 84 and 169).

Underpinning this process of gradual metamorphosis and variation is a tonal structure that – more than anything else – gives to the ballades their overall coherence and goal-directed momentum. A conspicuous feature of this tonal organisation is the preference for third-related regions. In the first two ballades the major third is the main tonal foundation: I–VI in No. 1; I–III in No. 2. In the last two ballades IV (third-related to VI) is also prominent: I–VI–IV in No. 3; I–IV–VI in No. 4. There are of course ample precedents for such tonal plans in the classical repertory (Beethoven, Schubert) and more particularly in the post-classical repertory (Hummel, Field). But the consistency across all four ballades is striking. And an important perspective on these relationships is their *avoidance* of the more conventional V.

I have commented elsewhere on Chopin's attitude to the dominant.[15] His avoidance of V as a means of articulating major formal successions (on a middleground level) is the more striking because he employs it so liberally on a foreground level, where it is largely without tonal significance,[16] and also on a background level, where it is powerfully structural. On the background level of the ballades Chopin's strategy is not so much to avoid the structural V as to postpone it until the latest possible stage of the argument.[17]

This brings me to the most fundamental of all the transformations of the sonata-form schema in the ballades. In all four works the overall progression of the work is towards a structural V which follows rather than precedes the restatement of the main themes. The one exception is No. 3 where there is no closing section and the structural V comes at the beginning of the reprise of Theme I. This is an important dimension of the 'plot' of the works in that the thematic reprise is not yet a synthesis, nor indeed a means of resolving the major tensions built up during the piece. We may note, for instance, that in No. 1 the reprise of Theme I is in its tension-building form over a dominant pedal and that the structural V occurs after it and immediately before the closing section. Theme I is in reality presented as a V$^6_4$ harmony which resolves to V$^5_3$ at bar 207 and to the tonic at the beginning of the closing section.

In No. 2 there is a similar pattern, with the V$^6_4$ harmony arriving at bar 157, the V$^5_3$ at 165 and the I at the beginning of the closing section. In No. 3 the procedure is more elliptical, but in essence the same. Here the V$^6_4$ prepares A♭ minor rather than major, as from 209. The arrival of the V$^5_3$ coincides with the reprise of Theme I (bar 213) while the I (major) is reached in the second bar of the theme. This makes sense retrospectively of the very opening bars of the work, where a straightforward reference to the tonic triad is conspicuously avoided. In No. 4 the arrival of the structural V is the most dramatic of all. Here V$^6_4$ is reached at 195 and V$^5_3$ at bar 202. The structural V is then prolonged by a succession of chords and resolves to I again at the beginning of the closing section at 211.

Further parallels in underlying tonal structure are revealed when we consider the route to the structural V. The four harmonic reductions (Exx. 24–7) which are used to illustrate these parallels are based on the ideas and methods of Schenker, as briefly outlined in Chapter 2 Note 3. The reductions indicate that in each case the approach to V is by way of its upper neighbour VI.[18] Indeed VI plays a critical role in controlling much of the larger harmonic movement in each ballade. In No. 1 the E♭ major of Theme II, initially a substitute for B♭ major, is firmly clinched at bar 138 and controls the entire succession until the V$^6_4$ at 194, as Schenker's graph indicates.

The later stages of the succession are presented as Ex. 24, essentially Schenker's graph, but presented again here to facilitate comparison with the structural harmonies of the three later ballades. My only gloss on the Schenker (the $^{6-5}_{4-3}$ preceding the closing section) is included simply to reinforce the similarity in underlying tonal structure between the four works. This is immediately apparent when we turn to the Second Ballade. There is of course a debate throughout the early stages of this work between F major and A minor, but with the establishment of A minor as the probable goal (we lose sight of the tonal starting point following the alternative dominants of 115–32), the F major may be viewed retrospectively as an upper neighbour to V

Example 24. Structural harmonies, First Ballade

Example 25. Structural harmonies, Second Ballade

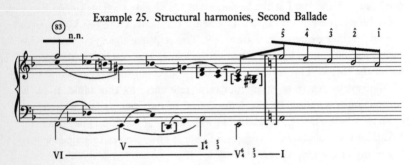

Example 26. Structural harmonies, Third Ballade

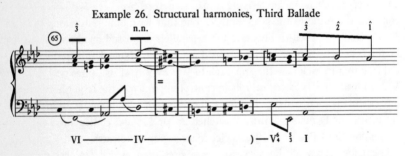

Example 27. Structural harmonies, Fourth Ballade

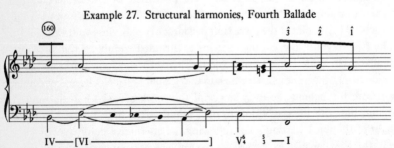

in A minor. Ex. 25 graphs the later stages as interpreted in relation to an A minor tonic.

In No. 3 the VI first appears with Theme II. It is given considerable structural weight on this appearance, and in a sense it remains suspended, merely reverting back to the A♭ tonic, which becomes in turn V of D♭ (C♯) minor (IV). It is a matter for argument to what extent the F continues to control subsequent events, but its weight in the structure is not in question. A diagram of the voice-leading at this background level helps make this clear (Ex. 26). In No. 4 this process is neatly reversed in that the first statement of Theme II is in IV and the second in VI. Here the relative loss of weight for VI (it is perceived as a substitute for a carefully prepared IV) is compensated by its proximity to the structural V to which it acts as a neighbour (Ex. 27).

It is apparent then that the foreground parallels between the ballades are strengthened by a more fundamental background parallel. Each ballade transforms the sonata-form archetype in such a way that the resolution of tonal tension is delayed until the latest possible moment, usually after the thematic reprise. And each finds its way to that resolution by a strikingly similar harmonic route. The bravura closing sections function then as a catharsis, releasing in a torrent of virtuosity all the tension which has been steadily mounting through the piece. It is to these larger tonal strategies that we must look to find the most compelling of all the cyclic links between the four ballades. Fundamentally each is a variation on a single structural pattern.

Narratives

Chorley's remark of 1834 may be recalled at this stage: 'We have always valued instrumental music as it has *spoken to us*, and can never listen to the delightful works of Beethoven, Mozart, Haydn, Ries, Onslow, and some others, without having their sentiment – nay, when we are in a fanciful humour – their *story*, as clearly impressed upon our minds as if it had been told in words.' No doubt Chorley's reference to sentiment and story related as much to a receding affective aesthetic as to an emergent expressive aesthetic, but it raised an issue – the semantic possibilities of music – which would recur often enough in later nineteenth-century criticism. This issue was suppressed to an extent by the Formalism of our own century, but it has resurfaced again in a recent body of literature dealing with music and narrative, much of it exploring applications from literary theory. We may in the end conclude, with Nattiez, that the term 'narrative' is inappropriately used of musical discourse,[19] or, with Carolyn Abbate, that it should be reserved for highly specific (and rarely occurring) musical gestures.[20] But given that the term *has* been used since the earliest critical commentaries on the ballades, it may be interesting to test its possible meanings.

If nothing else the genre title invites a narrative 'listening strategy'. The slow compound duple metre has suggested to many a narrating manner, even if what is being narrated remains unclear.[21] The reasons for this association are not obvious, though they will be touched upon shortly. In any event the association is well established, and it is no doubt partly in this sense that Serge Gut describes the Introduction and Theme I of the G minor ballade as in 'narrative' (time-dependent) mode, as opposed to the 'lyric' (time-neutralising) mode of Theme II.[22] The developmental restatements of the two themes (bars 94–125) are then described as 'narrative-epic' and 'lyric-epic' and the central sections (126–65) and coda as 'dramatic-virtuosic' and 'dramatic'. In this way a programme of sorts is assembled, with the symmetrical tonal design giving special privilege to the 'epic' material, allowing it to form a central axis in the progression from a narrative to a dramatic mode. Despite the distinguished ancestry and powerful resonance of these categories in literary poetics, they remain highly generalised as descriptions of musical events. They are incapable of sustaining the generic meaning which attaches to them in literature (stemming initially from Aristotle) and are in the end valuable only as a metaphor, a way of 'making available' our responses to a (purely) musical argument.

This is no less true of Eero Tarasti's much more ambitious attempt to devise a narratology for Chopin. In his study of the Polonaise-fantaisie Tarasti locates 'the concrete psychological contents' of the work in a series of 'successive narrative programmes'.[23] He takes this approach very much further in his study of the G minor Ballade, identifying fundamental modalities ('être', 'faire', 'devenir') and secondary modalities ('vouloir', 'savoir', 'pouvoir', 'devoir', 'croire') and applying these to the segmented events of the piece.[24] For all the sophistication of Tarasti's presentation, his analysis, like Gut's, relies on intuitive and largely subjective criteria both for the segmentation of the work and for the characterisation of its segments in terms of psychological states. This is not to deny the evocative quality of his modalities, nor their helpful contextual resonance. But it is not obvious that a series of modalities constitutes a narrative, any more than a succession of unrelated snapshots constitutes a film. Tarasti's exercise in reality comes closer to phenomenology than to narratology, in its fine-tuning and categorising – in terms of psychological values – what are presumed to be intersubjective responses to a play of forms.

Anthony Newcomb's contributions to the literature on music and narrative move a stage beyond the presentation of putative literary or psychological categories, recognising that an essential dimension of narrative is the establishment of causal relations between events presented in temporal succession.[25] Newcomb, withdrawing a semantic element entirely, refers to the 'paradigmatic plots' or 'plot archetypes' identified in the analyses of Russian folktales by Propp and of Theban myths by Levi-Strauss, and he suggests that in music too we 'follow the story' in relation to conventional formal successions. Setting aside the question of how we classify conventional successions (which need not be congruent with formal models such as sonata form), I will explore some implications of Newcomb's approach by way of a return to the question of norms and deviations. In addition to (and related to) their expressive potential, deviations from conventional models have a direct bearing on our perception of the temporal succession of musical ideas. Such deviations become in a sense special 'events', in that they modify the *implied* succession and are at the same time interpreted in relation to that implied succession. Their very unpredictability promotes 'active' listening in which we 'follow' the linear sequence of distinctive events, as we might the events in a dramatic plot. As Abbate puts it, the music 'mimes a drama'.

Yet Abbate's remark embodies a critique of this approach. Since music mimes or traces the drama – without discursive distance – it cannot narrate. 'Music dances to plots given to her from elsewhere.'[26] Abbate is no doubt right to deprive the compositional and listening strategies outlined by Newcomb of the status of narrative. For the moment I shall keep the metaphor of narrative at bay and look again at the strategies in their own terms. There is special point in doing so in relation to an early nineteenth-century repertory, since composers of Chopin's generation were characteristically concerned to project new thoughts against the backcloth of a classical heritage.

The conventional model invoked in the Third Ballade, for instance, is a sonata allegro, but the drama of the work unfolds through repeated deviations from the succession implied both by the model and by the nature of the musical materials themselves. The events, it should be stressed, are musical functions and need not be ascribed a semantic value. On the broadest scale they include the successive stages of an unorthodox tonal sequence (Theme I closes on I rather than V; Theme II settles in VI rather than V; the middle section opens with an extended stable section in I rather than a modulating section). And they include the successive stages by which conventional formal functions are recontextualised (the end of the exposition gives way to a stable episode rather than a development; the development appears in the course of, rather than before, the reprise; the work ends with an entirely unexpected return of Theme III).

In the classical sonata too there are deviations from a schema, but they tend to operate at a level of detail which leaves the larger conventional succession intact. The drama is perceived in part as a ritual, whose larger outcome is known in advance. In the Chopin ballade, on the other hand, the schema is repeatedly invoked only to be repeatedly subverted. And since the outcome of the drama cannot be safely predicted (even though it follows certain known lines), we perceive its unfolding as an event-series. The distinction in perception noted here is anything but absolute – there are no precise historical divisions – but it is real and pertinent, nonetheless, and it carries special relevance to the ballades. In remarking it, however, I am still fighting shy of the metaphor of narrative. As Abbate argues, 'there is more to narrating than mere reordering'.

I will brave the metaphor once again in order to note that an event-series will be focused by the characterisation and transformation of themes and by their interaction. All four ballades are in a sense 'about' two principal themes. Here too a parallel with the classical sonata is instructive. Where the normal practice of the classical sonata is to separate out the themes in the reprise, presenting them in more or less their original form (albeit in a tonal synthesis), the normal practice of the Chopin ballades is very different. Here the themes interact dramatically in the course of the work and are in the end transformed (often in an apotheosis). As Witten observes, it would be difficult to imagine them returning to their origins.[27] This in turn encourages us to hear them not just as components of a structure, but as proponents of a drama. They function as 'virtual agents' (Edward T. Cone's term to describe the imaginary participants of an instrumental drama), symbolically conveying the message of a 'virtual persona', who is by no means to be identified with the 'composer's persona'.[28]

The characterisation of themes, mainly through their links with popular genres, fosters this view of them as 'virtual agents' in a drama, preserving a sense of stylistic difference, even of disjunction. The range of events in an event-series might therefore be widened to include the successive stages of a changing sequence of distinctive styles. It is through this same disjunctive technique, though on a much simpler level, that the musical narrative of early nineteenth-century battle pieces in the popular repertory tends to be established, and it is perhaps not surprising that nineteenth-century critics sought similar semantic possibilities in the ballades. As Edward Dannreuther remarked of No. 2, 'One longs for a clue to the mysterious tale which the music unfolds.'[29] Such a remark hinges on the personification of themes as virtual agents, a device that is entirely explicit in Berlioz and Liszt, but remains implicit in Chopin. When the first theme of No. 2 returns at the end of the work, it has indeed assumed – as Anselm Gerhard observes – something of the character of an *idée fixe*.[30]

We are left with a not unimportant question. Who narrates Dannreuther's 'mysterious tale'? If a tale is narrated, rather than a drama mimed, there must be a voice outside the action recalling the events in the past tense.[31] It is in part this difficulty which leads Abbate to reject the narrative status of event-sequences and dramatic plots (to say nothing of the interpretative licence these permit). But music can arguably mimic the narrating voice. By introducing the concept of 'virtuality', Edward T. Cone (anticipating Seymour Chatman's 'implied narrator')[32] allows us to view even an instrumental work as an enactment, where a number of virtual agents – or a single agent – gives utterance to the message of a 'virtual persona'. Carolyn Abbate has on one level widened the scope of Cone's work, replacing his single experiencing and communicating subject with 'multiple, decentred voices'. On another level she has deliberately narrowed that scope by defining the narrating voice as special – particular to certain isolated and specific musical gestures. For Abbate the metaphor of a single narrating voice telling the story of a work would be implausible and unhelpful.

All the same it is that metaphor to which I stubbornly return in relation to the ballades. It has been argued here that the genre title encourages us to locate an unfolding story; that a story is more than a series of responses; that the ballades take on a story-character by invoking and then modifying conventional plots; that their events are focused through distinctive thematic characterisation; that in the end none of this adds up to a narrative, since we lack the discursive distance of a narrating voice. I will make one final attempt to justify the metaphor of narrative by seeking just such a narrating voice in the ballades. In doing so I conjecture a link with the most obvious of all sources, the poetic ballad, whose revival (of the medieval-folk genre) in the early nineteenth century was familiar to Chopin through the ballads of Mickiewicz.

In a stimulating investigation of this issue Neil Witten quotes Albert Friedman's definition of the narrative basis of the folk ballad in the 1974 *Encyclopedia Britannica*. He goes on to examine Mickiewicz's particular approach to the genre and finally to outline parallels with the Chopin ballades.[33] Witten's discussion is perceptive, but its useful insights are diluted by an attempt to clinch the case in too many particulars. It is not helpful, for instance, to equate evasive openings in the ballades with Mickiewicz's narrative technique of retrospective knowledge, especially since such openings are by no means unique to the ballades. Nor is it useful to equate the compound duple metre with a 'dramatic present tense', for which no musical equivalent can plausibly exist. Witten also finds musical parallels for the rhetorical questionings, abrupt transitions and so-called incremental repetitions of the ballad tradition, and again his analysis would carry more weight if these were musical features unique to the ballades.

Yet the analogy should not be totally discarded for all that. At the very least it is tempting to make an association between the compound duple metre of all four ballades and the unidentified narrator of the poetic ballad. It is a strained analogy, perhaps, but a suggestive one, and it may well lie at the root of many informal descriptions of the 'narrative' manner of the ballades. It is obvious that a theme or figuration has no real identity separate from its rhythmic profile. But in the Chopin ballades an illusion of discursive distance is created nonetheless, since the same metre underlies the very different event-series of the four pieces. In each ballade the simple, steady (usually iambic) tread of the compound duple metre acts as a thread linking the events of an unfolding drama. As a foreground 'presence' the metre is especially prominent in the earlier, texturally uncluttered stages of the ballades, receding into the background at the more climactic, densely textured moments. To stretch our analogy to breaking point, the narrator (the steady rhythmic tread) remains detached and impersonal, essentially uninvolved in the portentous events he or she relates.

A poetic ballad is, however, a rather special kind of narrative, if indeed it is a narrative at all. It has been well observed[34] that ballads function as 'dramatic conversations or monologues that act out the story' and that a framing narrator remains in the background. They stand in short somewhere between drama and narrative. This observation might actually help us place the Chopin ballades in relation to music and narrative, lodging them in a specific corner of the field through their connection with the poetic ballad. They too, it might be argued, stand somewhere between drama and narrative. As in the folk ballad, or Mickiewicz's recreation of it, the characters (virtual agents) in the Chopin ballades act out their drama as projections of a narrating voice (virtual persona) which is discernible but unobtrusive, ready to step back and allow the drama to become immediate and real.

Again as in the poetic ballad the 'plot' of the Chopin ballades invariably culminates in a moment of shattering climactic tension before any resolution is possible, and in the process the personalities of virtual agents are transformed and usually enlarged. Such analogies may be difficult to substantiate, fanciful even, but they are somehow compelling. And they can arguably invest Schumann's reporting with more significance than a search for specific poetic referents for each of the ballades in turn. There could be no more appropriate description of the closing moments of a Chopin ballade than Friedman's account (quoted by Witten) of the final stages of the folk ballad, where 'a phrase or stanza is repeated several times with a slight but significant substitution, until at last the final revelatory substitution bursts the pattern, achieving a climax and with it a release of powerful tensions'.

Notes

1 Background

1 The arguments for this date for the First Ballade will be discussed in Chapter 2. There is no documentary evidence supporting a later date for the Scherzo, but several authorities now agree (on stylistic grounds) that the work was probably composed much later than 1830–1, the date traditionally assigned to it. The most recent thematic catalogue (Józef Chomiński and Dalila Turło, *Katalog Dzieł Fryderyka Chopina*, Kraków 1990) suggests 1833 for both works, though the Wessel bill of sale on which this date is based is not a reliable indicator of the date of composition.

2 The Two Polonaises Op. 26, composed in 1835, also mark a departure from these traditions. They are generically distinct from the polonaises of the Warsaw period.

3 For a comprehensive list of concerts see William G. Attwood, *Fryderyk Chopin: Pianist from Warsaw*, New York 1987, pp. 193–5.

4 The phrase is from Fétis's review of Chopin's first concert in Paris, *Revue musicale*, 3 March 1832.

5 There is an intriguing account, perhaps not entirely reliable, of Chopin playing Beethoven in Wilhelm von Lenz, *The Great Piano Virtuosos of Our Time*, tr. Philip Reder, London 1983, pp. 47–8 (originally published in German, 1872).

6 *The Athenaeum*, 22 January 1848.

7 The phrase is Dahlhaus's in 'Neo-Romanticism', *Between Romanticism and Modernism*, tr. Mary Whittall, Berkeley, Los Angeles and London 1980, p. 3 (originally published in German, 1974).

8 Both pianists gave a series of 'historical concerts' in 1837, Moscheles in London and Liszt in Paris.

9 *The Athenaeum*, 3 June and 8 July 1843.

10 References to a 'brilliant' manner go back to Brossard's dictionary of 1701. The 'brilliant style' is discussed in Koch's Lexicon of 1802 and elsewhere in the late eighteenth and early nineteenth centuries. In the early nineteenth century it was increasingly applied to the repertory of post-classical concert music. This repertory had a sharply defined and widely recognised individual profile in contemporary perceptions. It was described (and often decried) as a 'modern school' (*The Athenaeum*, 16 February 1839), whose sole object seemed to be 'to play the greatest number of notes in a given time'(*The Musical World*, 15 July 1836), in contrast to the 'grave and well considered works of Steibelt, Dussek, Clementi and Woelfl and the more thoughtful and less mechanical creations of Beethoven and Weber' (*The Athenaeum*, 26 February 1842).

11 Chopin spent some time at Antonin, a summer home of Prince Radziwiłł, between his two visits to Vienna. He played the piano with the Prince's daughters and composed several works for the family.

12 See *The Journal of Eugène Delacroix*, London 1951, ed. Hubert Wellington, pp. 95–6. The discussions took place during 1849.

13 This issue is examined at length in John Rink, 'Chopin's "Structural Style" and its Relation to Improvisation', unpubl. diss., University of Cambridge 1989. See also Rink's chapter in *The Cambridge Companion to Chopin*, ed. Jim Samson, Cambridge 1992.

14 See the analysis of the B♭ minor Sonata in Józef Chomiński, *Sonaty Chopina*, Kraków 1960. See also several source studies of the Polonaise–fantaisie: Wojciech Nowik, 'Proces twórczy Fryderyka Chopina w świetle jego autografów muzycznych', unpubl. diss., University of Warsaw 1978; Jeffrey Kallberg, 'Chopin's Last Style', *Journal of the American Musicological Society*, 38, 1985, pp. 264–315; and Jim Samson, 'The Composition-draft of the Polonaise–fantaisie: the Issue of Tonality', *Chopin Studies*, ed. Jim Samson, Cambridge 1988, pp. 41–58.

15 To generalise drastically on this point: Liszt's inclination was to combine melody and figuration, surrounding the former with the latter. Chopin, on the other hand, tended to separate out the melody and figuration, presenting them in juxtaposition rather than superimposition.

16 I have discussed this at length in 'Chopin and Genre', *Music Analysis*, 8:3, October 1989, pp. 213–31.

17 For an examination of the shading between figuration, motive and harmony at the opening of the work see Jim Samson, *The Music of Chopin*, London, New York and Melbourne 1985, p. 161.

18 See Anthony Newcomb, 'Once More Between Absolute and Programme Music', *19th-Century Music*, 7, 1984, pp. 233–50 and 'Schumann and Late Eighteenth-Century Narrative Strategies', *19th-Century Music*, 11, 1987, pp. 164–74. Newcomb makes a useful distinction between formal archetypes, such as sonata form, and 'plot archetypes', which describe certain conventional narrative successions in eighteenth- and nineteenth-century music.

19 See Samson, 'Chopin and Genre'.

20 The earlier dictionaries, such as Koch's *Musikalisches Lexikon* (1802) and Gollmick's *Kritische Terminologie für Musiker und Musikfreunde* (1833), tend to describe the Ballade as a dance song, derived from the Italian Ballata. One commentator, Wiesław Lisecki, argues (unconvincingly) for Chopin's use of the term in this sense ('Die Ballade von Frederic Chopin – literarische oder musikalische Inspirationen', *Chopin Studies 3*, Warsaw 1990, pp. 305–18). Slightly later dictionaries, such as Schilling's *Universal-Lexicon der Tonkunst* (1835), refer also to the 'modern' use of the term as a category of art-song.

21 As, for instance, Wessel's advertisement for Ballades Nos. 1 and 2 in *The Musical Examiner*, 11 March 1843.

22 The issue is discussed in relation to Op. 38 in Anselm Gerhard, 'Ballade und Drama: Frederic Chopins Ballade opus 38 und die französische Oper um 1830', *Archiv für Musikwissenschaft*, 48:2, 1991, pp. 110–25.

23 *The Athenaeum*, 15 March, 1834. (Chorley's italics).

24 See, for example, Koczwara's *The Battle of Prague* and Challoner's *The Battle of Waterloo*.

25 An amusing, though much later, example of this genre is the twelve-part serial 'In the Ranks', published in Volume 1 of *The Musical Home Journal*, 1905.

26 Schumann, *Gesammelte Schriften über Musik und Musiker*, Leipzig 1854, repr. Wiesbaden 1985, Vol 4, p. 57.

27 Camille Bourniquel, *Chopin*, tr. Sinclair Road, New York and London, 1960 (originally published in French, 1957).

28 Frederick Niecks, *Chopin as a Man and a Musician*, London 1888, repr.1973, Vol. 2, p. 269.

29 Gerhard, 'Ballade und Drama'.

30 This was one of the most plundered of all operas by pianists of the time. There are arrangements by, among others, Valentin (a *siciliano* of similar character to Theme I of Op. 38), Kalkbrenner, Pixis, Chaulieu and Moscheles. The Ballade in Act I was transcribed for piano by Adolphe Adam.

31 Two-key schemes are also found in the popular domestic repertory. See, for instance, Challoner's *The Battle of Waterloo*.

32 This is reported in Jeffrey Kallberg, 'The Chopin Sources: Variants and Versions in Later Manuscripts', unpubl. diss., University of Chicago, 1982.

33 It is entirely typical of Chopin's music during these years that its relatively stable stylistic framework in no way prevented individual works forging their own highly distinctive sound worlds. It is enough to consider in tandem the opening themes of the Third Ballade and of the Third Scherzo, the one looking towards Schubert, the other towards Liszt.

34 This is discussed at length in Jeffrey Kallberg's review of Attwood, 'The Lioness and the Little One', *19th-Century Music*, 5, 1982, pp. 244–7.

35 This is detailed in a letter of June 1841. See *Selected Correspondence of Fryderyk Chopin*, tr. and ed. Arthur Hedley, London 1962, pp. 195–6 (based on *Korespondencja Fryderyka Chopina*, ed. B. E. Sydow, Warsaw 1955).

36 Kallberg's phrase with reference to the very final stages of Chopin's output. See 'Chopin's Last Style', pp. 264–315.

2 Genesis and reception

1 George Sand, *Histoire de ma vie, Oeuvres autobiographiques*, ed. Georges Lubin, 2 Vols., Paris 1978, Vol. 2, p. 446.

2 Maurice J. E. Brown, in *Chopin: An Index of his Works in Chronological Order* (London 1960, rev.1972), describes the incomplete manuscript of Op. 52 (No. 732 in Kobylańska, *Rękopisy Utworów Chopina*, Kraków 1977) as a sketch. This is just one example of a misunderstanding of Chopin's 'rejected public manuscripts'. There is an autograph fragment of Op. 38 (probably not part of a sketch) in the Museum of Music History, Stockholm; see Kobylańska No. 601.

3 Kallberg's term in 'The Chopin Sources'.

4 Kallberg's two articles 'Chopin in the Market-place' (Notes, 39:3 and 4, March and June 1983) offer the most comprehensive discussion to date of Chopin and his publishers.

5 See Kallberg, 'Chopin in the Market-place'.

6 For details of these pupils and of the annotated scores see J-J. Eigeldinger, *Chopin: Pianist and Teacher*, tr. Naomi Shohet, ed. Roy Howat, Cambridge 1986 (originally published as *Chopin vu par ses élèves*, Neuchâtel 1979).

7 Often the annotations were clearly for pedagogical reasons particular to the pupil in question.

8 In 'Die Ballade von Frederic Chopin', Wiesław Lisecki not only accepts the earlier date, but makes major inferences about the waltz elements in Op. 23 based on the assumption that the work was begun in Vienna. The date of 1833 offered by Chomiński and Turło (*Katalog*) is based on unreliable evidence.

9 I am indebted to Jeffrey Kallberg for drawing my attention to this.

10 Currently in private hands (the family of the cellist, Gregor Piatigorsky) in the USA.

11 Baron Stockhausen was the Netherlands Ambassador in Paris.

12 Ekier, in his *Kommentarze zródlowe* (Critical Commentary) on the Ballades (Kraków 1970, p. 9) for the *Wydanie Narodowe* (National Edition), suspects Henryk Probst, the Breitkopf & Härtel agent.

13 In Ekier, *Kommentarze*, p. 14.

14 Kobylańska, *Katalog* No. 275.

15 Hedley (ed), *Selected Correspondence*, p. 165.

16 *Ibid.*, p. 182.

17 Currently in the Bibliothèque nationale (Mus. 107).

18 Translated as 'A Chopin M.S.: the F Major Ballade in the Making' in Camille Saint-Saëns, *Outspoken Essays on Music*, tr. Fred Rothwell, London 1922, repr. 1970.

19 Gutman was one of Chopin's favourite pupils, and in later life a prolific composer of salon pieces.

20 In Ekier, *Kommentarze*, p. 27.

21 See Eigeldinger, *Chopin: Pianist and Teacher*, p. 65.

22 Hedley (ed.), *Selected Correspondence*, p. 210.

23 A photograph is held in the Chopin Society, Warsaw (F. 1334).

24 A descendant of one of France's oldest and grandest aristocratic families.

25 Kallberg, 'The Chopin Sources', pp. 110–41.

26 See Ekier, *Kommentarze*, pp. 48–9 for the reasoning here.

27 Hedley (ed.), *Selected Correspondence*, pp. 225–6.

28 In the private collection of Rudolph Kallir in New York.

29 Kallberg, 'The Chopin Sources', p. 175.

30 Ekier, *Kommentarze*, p. 78.

31 Camille Saint-Saëns, 'A Chopin M.S.: the F Major Ballade in the Making'.

32 In the introduction to the Oxford Original Edition.

33 In her review of the *Wydanie Narodowe* in *Chopin Studies 2*, Warsaw 1987, pp. 7–20.

34 See the discussion in Eigeldinger, *Chopin: Pianist and Teacher*, pp. 200–11.
35 Debussy was, however, incapable of resisting additional expression marks, such as the *sonore* which accompanies the 'horn-call' motive from Op. 23.
36 Bronarski wrote extensively on Chopin's harmonic practice, notably in *Harmonik Chopina*, Warsaw 1935, a book heavily based on the theories of Hugo Riemann.
37 In her review of *Wydanie Narodowy* in *Chopin Studies 2*.
38 J. Kallberg, 'Are Variants a Problem? "Composer's Intentions" in Editing Chopin', *Chopin Studies 3*, Warsaw 1990, pp. 257–68.
39 Liszt remarked on the silence of the critics concerning Chopin's music in the *Revue et Gazette musicale de Paris*, 2 May 1841. He interpreted this as a sign of acceptance, 'comme si la posterité était venue'.
40 See Attwood, *Fryderyk Chopin: Pianist from Warsaw*, pp. 132, 183, 235 and 237.
41 *The Autobiography of Charles Hallé*, ed. Michael Kennedy, London 1972, p. 54 (first published 1896).
42 *The Musical Standard*, 21 July 1866.
43 *The Athenaeum*, 1 January 1842.
44 See Zofia Chechlińska, 'Chopin Reception in Nineteenth-Century Poland' in *The Cambridge Companion to Chopin*, ed. Jim Samson. Documented performances of the ballades in the later nineteenth century include the Liszt pupil Hans von Bronsart playing Op. 47 in Leipzig (1857), Alfred Jaell (also a Liszt pupil) playing Op. 23 in Vienna (1859), William Mason playing Op. 47 in Vienna (1862) and von Bülow playing Op. 23 in an all-Chopin recital in London (1875). See George Kehler, *The Piano in Concert*, New Jersey and London 1982.
45 *La France musicale*, 9 May 1841.
46 James Huneker, *Mezzotints in Modern Music*, New York 1899, p. 165.
47 Moritz Karasowski describes the difficulties critics had with Op. 52 in *Frederic Chopin, His Life, Letters and Works*, tr. Emily Hill, New York 1878, p. 402. (originally published in German, 1877).
48 Karasowski (*ibid.*, p. 402) remarks that 'they contain so much that is new and varied in form that critics long hesitated to what category they should assign them'.
49 Neil Witten ('The Chopin "Ballades": An Analytical Study', unpubl. diss., Boston University 1974), seems unaware that in quoting Jachimecki's programme for Op. 38 and Perry's for Op. 47, he is referring to the same poem by Mickiewicz.
50 Jan Kleczyński, *Chopin's Greater Works*, tr. Natalie Janota, London 1896, p. 68 (originally published in Polish, 1886).
51 Félicien Mallefille used the term in a published letter to Chopin. See Kallberg, 'The Chopin Sources', pp. 99–100.
52 *Edinburgh Evening Courant*, 7 October 1848.
53 Félicien Mallefille, quoted in Józef Chomiński, *Fryderyk Chopin*, Leipzig 1980, p. 99.
54 Kleczyński, *Chopin's Greater Works*, p. 66.
55 G. C. Ashton Jonson, *A Handbook to Chopin's Works*, London 1905, p. 76.
56 Kleczyński, *The Works of Frederic Chopin and their Proper Interpretation*, tr. Alfred Whittingham, London 1913, p. 17 (originally published in Polish, 1879).

57 Louis Ehlert, *Aus der Tonwelt*, Berlin 1877, p. 298.

58 Karasowski, *Frederic Chopin*, p. 402.

59 *The Musical Standard*, 17 October 1848.

60 *Le Ménestrel*, 2 May 1841.

61 *La France musicale*, 2 May 1841.

62 *La France musicale*, 27 May 1842.

63 Hippolyte Barbedette, *Chopin: Essai de Critique Musicale*, Paris 1869, p. 71.

64 Mallefille, quoted in Chominski, *Fryderyk Chopin*, p. 99.

65 *Revue et Gazette musicale de Paris*, 27 February 1842.

66 Schumann, *Gesammelte Schriften*, Vol. 4, pp. 55–7 and 193–4.

67 *The Musical Standard*, 21 July 1866.

68 *The Musical Examiner*, 4 February 1843.

69 *The Musical Examiner*, 18 March 1843.

70 *The Musical Examiner*, 4 March 1843.

71 *The Musical Examiner*, 31 December 1842.

72 Quoted in Frederick Niecks, *Chopin as a Man and a Musician*, Vol. 1, p. 269.

73 *The Athenaeum*, 26 February 1842.

74 See Charles Reid, *The Music Monster*, London 1984, p. 149.

75 *Ibid.*, pp. 26–30.

76 *The Autobiography of Charles Hallé*, p. 54.

77 *The Athenaeum*, 2 February 1839.

78 Henry Hadow, *Studies in Modern Music: Second Series*, London 1926, p. 157.

79 Hubert Parry, *The Art of Music*, London 1905, p. 299.

80 Bernard Scharlitt, *Chopin*, Leipzig 1919.

81 *Shaw's Music 1890–1893*, ed. Dan H. Lawrence, The Bodley Head Bernard Shaw, London, Sydney and Toronto 1981, p. 762.

82 Hugo Leichtentritt, *Analyse der Chopinschen Klavierwerke*, 2 Vols., Berlin 1921.

83 There were isolated instances of this in the nineteenth century (Anton Rubinstein, Marx–Goldschmidt and Busoni). It became more popular in the 1920s and 1930s, with cycles given by Risler, Cortot, Ciampi and Casadesus. For details see Kehler, *The Piano in Concert*.

84 Jan Ekier, 'How Did Chopin Play?'. A paper read to the Chopin Symposium, Warsaw 1986.

85 Several eighteenth-century sources examine types of tempo fluctuation. The matter is discussed in David Rowland, 'Chopin's *Tempo Rubato* in Context', *Chopin Studies 2*, ed. John Rink and Jim Samson, Cambridge, forthcoming.

86 For a selection see Eigeldinger, *Chopin: Pianist and Teacher*, pp. 267–95.

87 See the section on the 'brilliant style' in C. F. Weitzmann, *A History of Pianoforte Playing and Pianoforte Literature*, New York 1897, repr. 1969.

88 See *Hanslick's Music Criticisms*, tr. Henry Pleasants, London 1950, repr. New York 1988, pp. 49–50.

89 See James Methuen-Campbell, *Chopin Playing: From the Composer to the Present Day*, London 1981.

90 There is an evocative description of Tausig's interpretation of the Fourth Ballade

in von Lenz, *The Great Piano Virtuosos of Our Time*, pp. 72–4.

91 Quoted in Methuen-Campbell, 'Chopin in Performance: From the Composer to the Present Day', *The Cambridge Companion to Chopin*, ed. Jim Samson.

92 See Reginald Gerig, *Famous Pianists and Their Technique*, New York 1974.

93 There is an interesting account of Hofmann's very different, highly expressive, reading of this section in Abram Chasins, *Speaking of Pianists*, New York 1957, p. 32.

94 Eigeldinger, *Chopin: Pianist and Teacher*, p. 276.

3 Form and design

1 Alan Rawsthorne, 'Ballades, Fantasy and Scherzos', *Frederic Chopin: Profiles of the Man and the Musician*, ed. Alan Walker, London 1966, pp. 42–72.

2 For a discussion of octatonic writing in Chopin see Roy Howat, 'Chopin's Influence on the *Fin de Siècle* and Beyond' in *The Cambridge Companion to Chopin*, ed. Jim Samson, Cambridge 1992.

3 Heinrich Schenker, *Free Composition*, tr. and ed. Ernst Oster, New York and London 1979, Vol. 2, Fig. 153 (originally published in German, 1935). Schenker's work is based on the premise that the masterpieces of tonal composition are based on a hierarchy of interdependent structural levels, ranging from the Fundamental Structure and the 'background' level (in which a simple harmonic progression (I–V–I) in the bass accompanies a contrapuntal linear descent in the treble, known as the Fundamental Line) to increasingly complex elaborations and 'prolongations' of this remote structure at 'middleground' and 'foreground' levels. It is in this sense that the terms 'foreground', 'middleground' and 'background' are used in this book. Schenker's analyses (known as 'graphs') are invariably presented as harmonic reductions designed to reveal the essential structural harmonies of a work. Even without a detailed understanding of the method, it should be possible to grasp the underlying sense of a Schenkerian analysis by comparing these reductions with the score. Terminology such as 'Fundamental Line' and 'structural V' (referring to the background level) is used from time to time in this book.

4 The term 'coda' is inappropriate for these sections of the ballades.

5 Anatoly Leikin, 'The Dissolution of Sonata Structure in Romantic Piano Music (1820–1850)', unpubl. diss., University of California (Los Angeles) 1986, pp. 253–6.

6 Witten, 'The Chopin "Ballades"', pp. 27–31.

7 Hugo Leichtentritt, *Analyse von Chopinschen Klavierwerke*, Vol. 2, p. 7.

8 Witten ('The Chopin "Ballades"', p. 63) makes a useful parallel with the 'closing theme' in Op. 58.

9 Wai-Ling Cheong, 'Structural Coherence and the Two-Key Scheme: A Study of Selected Cases from the Nineteenth Century', unpubl. diss., University of Cambridge, 1988, pp. 41–58.

10 See Witten, 'The Chopin "Ballades"', p. 141.

11 See Schumann, *Gesammelte Schriften*, Vol. 4, pp. 55–7.

12 Gerald Abraham, *Chopin's Musical Style*, London 1939, 2nd edn. 1941, pp. 56–7. See also Edward Zolas, 'A Study and Recital of the Four Ballades of Frederic Chopin', unpubl. diss. Columbia University 1983, pp. 35–6.

13 See, for example, William Kinderman, 'Directional Tonality in Chopin', in *Chopin Studies*, ed. Jim Samson, Cambridge 1988, pp. 59–76.

14 *Free Composition*, Vol. 2, Fig. 13.

15 Carl Schachter, 'The Fantasy Op. 49: The Two-Key Scheme' in *Chopin Studies*, ed. Jim Samson, pp. 221–53.

16 There is some empirical support for this. See Nicholas Cook, *Music, Culture and Imagination*, Oxford 1991, pp. 52–7.

17 It has already been noted that two-key schemes were far from unknown in the repertory of post-classical concert music, which formed the stylistic foundations for Chopin's mature music.

18 *Journal of Music Theory*, 25:1, 1981, pp. 1–16.

19 Kevin Korsyn, 'Directional Tonality and Intertextuality: A Comparison of Chopin's Ballade, Op. 38, with the Second Movement of Brahms's Quintet, Op. 88', paper read to the conference Alternatives to Monotonality, University of Victoria, February 1989.

20 Charles Rosen, *Sonata Forms*, New York and London 1980, pp. 295–6.

21 Graham George, *Tonality and Musical Structure*, London 1970.

22 Much of Bailey's work remains unpublished. For a bibliography which includes unpublished papers see Christopher Orlo Lewis, *Tonal Coherence in Mahler's Ninth Symphony*, Ann Arbor 1984, p. 125.

23 See note 13.

24 Stephen Emmerson, 'Progammatic and Symbolic References in the Early Music of Bartók', unpubl. diss., University of Oxford 1989.

25 I am grateful to Professor Krebs for allowing me to see a manuscript of his book.

26 Witten, 'The Chopin "Ballades"', pp. 347–55.

27 See, for example, the discussion in Witten, *ibid.*, p. 187ff.

28 I have described and illustrated this process in *The Music of Chopin*, p. 185.

29 For example, by Rawsthorne in 'Ballades, Fantasy and Scherzos'.

30 See Leikin, 'The Dissolution of Sonata Structure', pp. 217–29

31 See Wladimir Protopopow, 'Polifonia w *Balladzie f-moll* Chopina', *Rocznik Chopinowski*, 7, Warsaw 1969, pp. 34–44.

32 In a review of my book *The Music of Chopin* in *Music Analysis*, 8:1/2, March/July 1989, pp. 187–97.

4 Genre

1 Much of the material in this section is based on my article 'Chopin and Genre'.

2 See Franco Fabbri, 'A Theory of Musical Genre: Two Applications', *Popular Music Perspectives*, ed. Philip Tagg and David Horn, Goteborg and Exeter 1982, pp. 52–81.

3 The phrase is Schlovsky's. See also Boris Tomaschevsky, 'Literary Genres', tr. L.

M. O'Toole, *Formalism: History, Comparison, Genre*, ed. L. M. O'Toole and Ann Shukman, Oxford 1978, pp. 52–93 (originally published in Russian, 1928).

4   It is tempting to compare Chopin's transformation of post-classical concert music with Lermontov's transformation of Russian poetry in the 1820s, as described by Eikhenbaum, 'Some Principles of Literary History: The Study of Lermontov' in *Formalism: History, Comparison, Genre*, pp. 1–8.

5   See the chapter 'The Function of Genre' in Heather Dubrow, *Genre*, London 1982. Jeffrey Kallberg has developed this idea in several papers, notably 'Understanding Genre: A Reinterpretation of the Early Piano Nocturne', *Atti del XIV Congresso della Societa Internazionale di Musicologia*, Bologna 1987, pp. 775–9.

6   *Aesthetic Theory*, ed. Gretel Adorno and Rolf Tiedemann, tr. Christian Lenhardt, London 1984, p. 292.

7   I have examined this at length in 'Chopin's F-sharp Impromptu: Notes on Genre, Style and Structure', *Chopin Studies 3*, Warsaw 1990, pp. 297–304.

8   This model is examined in relation to the four impromptus in 'Chopin and Genre'.

9   'The Chopin "Ballades"', pp. 172–3 and 367.

10   *Classic Music: Expression, Form and Style*, New York and London 1980. Ratner uses the term 'topic' to identify the different stylistic and generic types available to classical composers. His 'topics' include dance types, such as sarabande or siciliano, as well as more generalised styles, such as the 'military' or the 'brilliant'.

11   Nor is there much evidence that 'ballades' by later composers validated Chopin's private definition of the genre. See G. Wagner, *Die Klavierballade um die Mitte des 19 Jahrhunderts*, Munich 1976.

12   'The Dissolution of Sonata Structure', pp. 219–29. Similar points are made by Mazel, *Issledovaniya o Shopene*, Moscow 1971, pp. 178–86, and Anna Bogdańska, 'Technika wariacyjna i praca tematyczna w balladach Chopina', *Rocznik Chopinowski*, 18, Warsaw 1986, pp. 63–90.

13   *Beyond Orpheus: Studies in Musical Structure*, Cambridge, Massachusetts and London 1979.

14   Bogdańska, 'Technika wariacyjna'.

15   *The Music of Chopin*, pp. 213–14.

16   Theme II of Op. 23 offers a good example of the characteristic enrichment of the chord members of a foreground progression by the 'application' of dominant seventh harmonies. I have analysed the harmonies here in detail in *The Music of Chopin*, pp. 177–8.

17   This point has been made by several commentators, but most cogently by Witten, 'The Chopin "Ballades"', pp. 365–70.

18   This is also noted by Witten, *ibid.*, pp. 365–70.

19   Jean-Jacques Nattiez, 'Can One Speak of Narrativity in Music?', *Journal of the Royal Musical Association*, 115:2, 1990, pp. 240–57.

20   Carolyn Abbate, *Unsung Voices: Opera and Musical Narrative in the Nineteenth Century*, Princeton 1991.

21   Almost all commentators refer to this, from Kleczyński, through Leichtentritt to Abraham and Rawsthorne.

22 Serge Gut, 'Interférences entre le langage et la structure dans la Ballade en sol-mineur Op. 23', paper read to the Chopin Symposium, Warsaw 1989.

23 Eero Tarasti, 'Pour une narratologie de Chopin', *International Review of Aesthetics and Sociology of Music*, 15, 1984, pp. 53–75.

24 Eero Tarasti, 'Sur la narrativité dans les Ballades de Chopin', paper read to the Chopin Symposium, Warsaw 1989.

25 See Chapter 1, note 18.

26 Abbate, *Unsung Voices*, p. 27.

27 Witten, 'The Chopin "Ballades"', pp. 386–7.

28 Edward T. Cone, *The Composer's Voice*, Berkeley, Los Angeles and London 1974.

29 In *The Romantic Period*, The Oxford History of Music, Vol. 6, Oxford 1905, p. 257.

30 Gerhard, 'Ballade und Drama', p. 122.

31 Both Nattiez ('Can One Speak of Narrativity in Music?') and Abbate (*Unsung Voices*) have drawn attention to this difficulty in making analogies between music and narrative.

32 Seymour Chatman, *Story and Discourse*, New York 1978.

33 'The Chopin "Ballades"', pp. 371–90.

34 Abbate, *Unsung Voices*, pp. 53–4.

Select bibliography

Abbate, Carolyn. *Unsung Voices: Opera and Musical Narrative in the Nineteenth Century* (Princeton 1991)

Abraham, Gerald. *Chopin's Musical Style* (London 1939, 2nd edn. 1941)

Ashton Jonson, G. C. *A Handbook to Chopin's Works* (London 1905)

Attwood, William G. *Fryderyk Chopin: Pianist from Warsaw* (New York 1987)

Barbedette, Hippolyte. *Chopin: Essai de Critique Musicale* (Paris 1869)

Bogdańska, Anna. 'Technika wariacyjna i praca tematyczna w balladach Chopina', *Rocznik Chopinowski*, 18 (Warsaw 1986) pp. 63–90

Bourniquel, Camille. *Chopin*, tr. Sinclair Road (New York and London 1960). Originally published in French, 1957

Brown, M. J. E. *Chopin: An Index of his Works in Chronological Order* (London 1960, rev. 1972)

Chasins, Abram. *Speaking of Pianists* (New York 1957)

Chatman, Seymour. *Story and Discourse* (New York 1978)

Chechlińska, Zofia. 'Chopin Reception in Nineteenth-Century Poland', *The Cambridge Companion to Chopin*, ed. Jim Samson (Cambridge 1992)

Cheong, Wai-Ling. 'Structural Coherence and the Two-Key Scheme: A Study of Selected Cases from the Nineteenth Century' (unpubl. diss., University of Cambridge 1988)

Chomiński, Józef. *Fryderyk Chopin* (Leipzig 1980)
     and Turło, Dalila. *Katalog Dzieł Fryderyka Chopina* (Kraków 1990)

Cone, Edward T. *The Composer's Voice* (Berkeley, Los Angeles and London 1974)

Ehlert, Louis. *Aus der Tonwelt* (Berlin 1877)

Eigeldinger, J.-J. *Chopin: Pianist and Teacher*, tr. Naomi Shohet, ed. Roy Howat (Cambridge 1986). Originally published in French, 1979

Ekier, Jan. *Ballady: Komentarze zródlowe* (Kraków 1970)
     Wstęp do Wydania Narodowego Dzieł Fryderyka Chopina (Kraków 1974)

Gerhard, Anselm. 'Ballade und Drama: Frederic Chopin Ballade opus 38 und die französische Oper um 1830', *Archiv für Musikwissenschaft*, 48 (1991), pp. 110–25

Gerig, Reginald. *Famous Pianists and Their Technique* (New York 1974)

Hadow, Henry. *Studies in Modern Music: Second Series* (London 1926)

Hedley, Arthur (tr. and ed.) *Selected Correspondence of Fryderyk Chopin* (London 1962)

Kallberg, Jeffrey. 'The Chopin Sources: Variants and Versions in Later Manuscripts' (unpubl. diss., University of Chicago 1982)
     'Chopin's Last Style', *Journal of the American Musicological Society*, 38 (1985), pp. 264–315
     'Chopin in the Market-place', *Notes*, 39:3 and 4 (1983), pp. 535–69, 795–824

'Are Variants a Problem? "Composer's Intentions" in Editing Chopin', *Chopin Studies 3* (Warsaw 1990), pp. 257–68

Kański, Jozef. *Dyskografia Chopinowska: Historyczny katalog nagrań plytowych* (Kraków 1986)

Karasowski, Moritz. *Frederic Chopin, His Life, Letters and Works*, tr. Emily Hill (New York 1878). Originally published in German, 1877

Kehler, George. *The Piano in Concert* (New Jersey and London 1982)

Kennedy, Michael (ed.). *The Autobiography of Charles Hallé* (London 1972). First published 1896

Kleczyński, Jan. *Chopin's Greater Works*, tr. Natalie Janota (London 1896). Originally published in Polish, 1886

Kobylańska, Krystyna. *Rękopisy Utworów Chopina* (Kraków 1977)

Krebs, Harald. 'Alternatives to Monotonality in early Nineteenth-century Music', *Journal of Music Theory*, 25:1 (1981), pp. 1–16

Leichtentritt, Hugo. *Analyse der Chopinschen Klavierwerke* (Berlin 1921)

Leikin, Anatoly. 'The Dissolution of Sonata Structure in Romantic Piano Music (1820–1850)' (unpubl. diss., University of California (Los Angeles) 1986)

Lenz, Wilhelm von. *The Great Piano Virtuosos of Our Time*, tr. Philip Reder (London 1983). Originally published in German, 1872

Lisecki, Wiesław. 'Die Ballade von Frederic Chopin – literarische oder musikalische Inspirationen', *Chopin Studies 3* (Warsaw 1990), pp. 305–18

Methuen-Campbell, James. *Chopin Playing: From the Composer to the Present Day* (London 1981)

Nattiez, J-J. 'Can One Speak of Narrativity in Music?', *Journal of the Royal Musical Association*, 115:2 (1990), pp. 240–57

Newcomb, Anthony. 'Once More "Between Absolute and Programme Music"', *19th-Century Music*, 7 (1984), pp. 233–50

'Schumann and Late Eighteenth-Century Narrative Strategies', *19th-Century Music*, 2 (1986), pp. 164–74

Niecks, Frederick. *Chopin as a Man and a Musician* (London 1888, repr. 1973)

Nowik, Wojciech. 'Proces twórczy Fryderyka Chopina w świetle jego autografów muzycznych' (unpubl. diss., University of Warsaw 1978)

Protopopow, Wladimir. 'Polifonia w *Balladzie f-moll* Chopin', *Rocznik Chopinowski*, 7 (Warsaw 1969) pp. 34–44

Rawsthorne, Alan. 'Ballades, Fantasy and Scherzos', *Frederic Chopin: Profiles of the Man and the Musician*, ed. Alan Walker (London 1966) pp. 42–72

Reid, Charles. *The Music Monster* (London 1984)

Rink, John. 'The Evolution of Chopin's "Structural Style" and its Relation to Improvisation' (unpubl. diss., University of Cambridge 1989)

Rosen, Charles. *Sonata Forms* (New York and London 1980)

Saint-Saëns, Camille. 'A Chopin M. S.: the F major Ballade in the Making', *Outspoken Essays on Music*, tr. Fred Rothwell (London 1922, repr. 1970)

Samson, Jim. *The Music of Chopin* (London, New York and Melbourne 1985)

(ed.), *Chopin Studies* (Cambridge 1988)

(ed.), *The Cambridge Companion to Chopin* (Cambridge 1992)

'Chopin and Genre', *Music Analysis*, 8:3 (1989), pp. 213–31

Sand, George. *Oeuvres autobiographiques*, ed. Georges Lubin (Paris 1978)

Schenker, Heinrich. *Free Composition*, tr. and ed. Ernst Oster (New York and London 1979). Originally published in German, 1935

Schumann, Robert. *Gesammelte Schriften über Musik und Musiker* (Leipzig 1854, repr. Wiesbaden 1985)

Tarasti, Eero. 'Pour une narratologie de Chopin', *International Review of Aesthetics and Sociology of Music*, 15 (1984), pp. 53–75

Wagner, G. *Die Klavierballade um die Mitte des 19 Jahrhunderts* (Munich 1976)

Walker, Alan (ed.). *Frederic Chopin: Profiles of the Man and the Musician* (London 1966)

Weitzmann, C. F. *A History of Pianoforte Playing and Pianoforte Literature* (New York 1897, repr. 1969)

Witten, Neil. 'The Chopin "Ballades": An Analytical Study' (unpubl. diss., Boston University 1974)

Zolas, Edward. 'A Study and Recital of the Four Ballades of Frederic Chopin' (unpubl. diss., Columbia University 1983)

Index

Abbate, C., 82–5
Abraham, G., 53
Adorno, T., 70–1
Allgemeine musikalische Zeitung, 35
Antonin, 5
Aristotle, 82
Arrau, C., 44
Ashdown & Perry, 26
Ashkenazy, V., 43
Athenaeum, 5, 35, 69
Augener & Co., 28

Bach, J. S., 4, 6, 19
Bacon, F., 36
Bailey, R., 55
Balakirev, M., 37
Bartók, B., 55
Beethoven, L. van, 4, 11, 78, 81
Bellamy, H., 32
Berlioz, H., 11–12, 36, 85
Bessel & Cie., 28
Biehl, E., 28
Bogdańska, A., 77
Bosworth & Co., 28
Bote & Bock, 28
Bourges, M., 35
Bourniquel, C., 15, 34
Bowerman & Co., 28
Brahms, J., 26, 36
Brandus, L. & G., 26
Breithaupt, R. M., 40

Breitkopf & Härtel, 20–4, 26, 30
Broadwood, J., 3
Bronarski, L., 30
Brugnoli, A., 30
Bulow, H. von, 36, 39

Carreño, T., 39–40, 4 3
Casadesus, R., 39, 44
Chatman, S., 85
Chechlińska, Z., 30–1
Cheong, W-L., 51
Cherubini, L., 17
Chopin, F., Works
  Variations Op. 2 *Là ci darem*, 2
  Sonata Op. 4, 2, 5, 8
  4 Mazurkas Op. 6, 5
  5 Mazurkas Op. 7, 5
  Piano Trio Op. 8, 2, 5, 8
  3 Nocturnes Op. 9, 5–6
  12 Etudes Op. 10, 5–6
  Variations brillantes Op. 12, 7
  Fantasy on Polish Airs Op. 13, 2
  Rondo à la Krakowiak Op. 14, 2
  Rondo Op. 16, 7, 53
  Waltz Op. 18, 9
  Bolero Op. 19, 53
  Scherzo Op. 20, 1, 3–5, 7–8
  12 Etudes Op. 25, 15–6
  24 Preludes Op. 28, 53
  4 Mazurkas Op. 30, 53
  Scherzo Op. 31, 53–5

3 Waltzes Op. 34, 9
2 Nocturnes Op. 37, 15
Scherzo Op. 39, 53
2 Nocturnes Op. 48, 60
Fantasy Op. 49, 23, 53–5
Impromptu Op. 51, 19
Polonaise Op. 53, 19
Berceuse Op. 57, 19
Barcarolle Op.6 0, 19
Polonaise-fantaisie Op. 61, 19, 82
3 Waltzes Op. 64, 3
Nocturne, E minor, 5
Chorley, H., 11, 35, 81
Cone, E. T., 84–5
Cortot, A., 19, 30, 34, 39, 41

Dannreuther, E., 85
Davison, J. W., 35–6
Debussy, C., 30
Delacroix, E., 6, 12
Deneke, M., 26
Deppe, L., 40
Dessauer, P., 25
Dubois, C. (O'Meara), 21
Durand & Cie., 30

Ehlert, L., 35
Eigeldinger, J-J., 31
Ekier, J., 22–6, 31, 38
Emmerson, S., 55
Epstein, D., 77
Erard, S., 3

Fétis, F-J., 26–7
Field, J., 5–6, 38, 78
Filtsch, C., 4
Fontana, J., 21–4, 26
Franchomme, A., 16, 24–5, 32
François, S., 39
Frankfurt School, 70
Friedman, A., 85, 87
Friedman, I., 30, 39–41

Ganche, E., 28, 30
Gebethner & Wolff, 28–9
Gerhard, A., 85
Grundgestalt, 77
Gut, S., 82
Gutman, A., 23

Hallé, C., 4–5, 39
Haydn, J., 11, 81
Hegel, G. W. F., 11
Henle Verlag, 31
Heugel & Cie., 28
Higgins, T., 31
Hoffmann, E. T. A., 12
Hofmann, J., 39, 43
Holmes & Karn, 32
Horkheimer, M., 70
Horowitz, V., 42
Houston, A. D., 30
Hummel, J. N., 3, 5, 16, 18–9, 38, 78
Huneker, J., 34

Iris, 35

Jean Paul, 12
Jędrzejewicz, L., 21, 23–4
Jurgenson, P., 27

Kalkbrenner, F., 16
Kallberg, J., 24–5
Karasowski, M., 35
Kastner, J-G., 17
Kinderman, W., 55
Kistner, F., 28
Kleczyński, J., 29, 34
Klindworth, K., 28
Kobylańska, K., 22, 25
Koczalski, R., 39, 41–4
Köhler, C. L. H., 28
Konneritz, R. de, 29
Korsyn, K., 54
Krebs, H., 54, 56

Index

Lamartine, H., 12–3, 35
Lea Pocket Scores, 26
Lebert, S., 40
Leichtentritt, H., 37
Leikin, A., 48, 77
Leschetizky, T., 38–42
Levi-Strauss, C., 83
Lhevinne, J., 39
Liszt, F., 3–4, 7, 11–2, 14, 26, 28, 35–6, 39, 55, 77–8, 85
Litolff, H., 28
Loewe, C., 11
Long, M., 39

Magaloff, N., 39
Marmontel, A., 28
Mathias, G., 29, 39
Matthay, T., 40
Meissonier et fils, 26
Mendelssohn, F., wife of, 26
Merrick, F., 32
Meyerbeer, G., 15–6
Michałowski, A., 39
Mickiewicz, A., 12, 16–7, 34, 85–6
Mikuli, K., 28–30, 39, 41–2
Milton, J., 36
Moiseiwitsch, B., 39, 42
Moscheles, I., 4, 24
Mozart, W. A., 4, 6, 11, 37, 81
Musical Standard, 35
Musical World, 35–6

Nattiez, J-J., 81
Neue Zeitschrift für Musik, 35
Neuhaus, H., 39
Newcomb, A., 75, 83
Niecks, F., 15, 37
Norwid, C., 12
Nouilles, P., 24
Novaes, G., 39
Novello & Co., 32

Onslow, G., 11, 81
Oxford Original Edition, 30

Pachmann, V. de, 40
Paderewski, I., 30, 39–40
Palmer, K., 32
Perlemuter, V., 39, 43
Peters, C. F., 29
Philipp, I., 39
Planté, F, 39
Pogorelich, I., 44
Polish National Edition, 32
Pollini, M., 43
Post-Structuralism, 71–2
Probst, H., 16
Propp, V., 83
Pugno, R., 30, 39

Rakhmaninov, S., 39–41
Ratner, L., 73
Rellstab, L., 35–6
Revue et Gazette musicale de Paris, 35
Richault & Cie., 26–7
Richebourg, E., 32
Richter, S., 44
Ricordi & Cie., 30
Riemann, H., 32, 37
Ries, F., 11, 81
Rosen, C., 39, 54–5
Rosenthal, M., 39
Rubinstein, Anton, 39
Rubinstein, Artur, 41–3
Russian Formalism, 69–72

Safonov, V., 39
Saint-Saëns, C., 22–4, 28
Salabert, E., 30
Sand, G., 17, 20
Sauer, E., 30, 39
Schachter, C., 54, 67
Scharlitt, B., 37

Scharwenka, X., 28
Schenker, H., 37, 48, 53–4, 79
Scherbatoff, M. de, 24
Schirmer inc., 28
Schlesinger, A. M., 26
Schlesinger, M., 20–2, 24, 26–7, 35
Schoenberg, A., 77
Scholtz, H., 29–30
Schonenberger, G., 26–7,
Schott, B. Söhne, 30
Schubert, F., 11, 17, 78
Schumann, C., 39
Schumann, R., 11–13, 16, 23, 34, 35, 53, 87
Shakespeare, W., 12
Shaw, G. B., 37
Sliwiński, J., 39
Sofronitsky, V., 39
Solomon, 42
Stark, L., 39

Stellowski, Th. & F., 27
Stirling, J., 21, 23–4, 27, 30
Stockhausen, Baron, 21

Tarasti, E., 82
Tausig, C., 39
Tellefsen, T., 26–7, 30
Troupenas & Cie., 23, 26
Turczyński, J., 30

Universal Edition, 30

Wagner, R., 36, 55
Weber, C. M. von, 5
Wessel & Co., 20–4, 26
Wiener Urtext, 31
Witten, N., 73, 84–7

Zimerman, K., 43–4
Zimmerman, E., 31